The Seven Steps To Finally Loving Yourself

How To Become Powerfully Confident, Let Go Of Your Fears, And Radically Transform Your Life

Copyright © 2018 Laurelle Burgham. All rights reserved. No portion of this book, except for brief review, may be reproduced, stored in a retrieval system, or transmitted in any form or by any means—electronic, mechanical, photocopying, recording, or otherwise—without the written permission of the publisher.

Published by

Inspired Publishing Ltd
27 Old Gloucester Street
London
WC1N 3AX

Printed in the United Kingdom

ISBN: 978-1-78555-083-6

Table of Contents

Foreword 1

Introduction 3

Chapter 1 – My Journey to Self-Love 9

Chapter 2 – The Meaning and Importance of Self-Esteem 15

Chapter 3 – How Self-Love Affects Your Life 31

Chapter 4 – Fear - And How to Overcome It 39

Chapter 5 – The Self-Love, Nutrition and Health Connection 49

Chapter 6 – How Your Relationships are Affected by Your Self-Love 65

Chapter 7 – How Advertising Exploits Your Emotional Vulnerabilities 73

Chapter 8 – Tools 87

Chapter 9 – How to Increase Your Self-Esteem 111

Chapter 10 – Meditating Your Way to Healthy Self-Esteem 131

Chapter 11 – How to Raise Your Vibrational Frequency and Transform Your Life 143

Conclusion 159

FOREWORD

Dear reader,

Congratulations on deciding to invest in yourself, for having an open mind, and for being willing to learn more about how you can start loving yourself, and your life again.

If you're reading these words, it means that you have already taken the first steps towards brightening your future and letting the light back into your life. I feel privileged to have the opportunity of reaching out to you through my book.

I want to put you at ease here: It is DEFINITELY possible for anybody to become more self-confident and to learn to love themselves, regardless of past traumatic experiences. If you start modeling what other confident people say, do, believe, and focus on, you absolutely can start making a difference in the way you're living your life, starting today.

The most successful and self-loving people out there all had to overcome personal battles and subconscious, limiting beliefs in order to be the great individuals they are today. They all had to deal with feelings of inadequacy, the exact things that stand between you and greatness right now.

What you need to achieve self-love and self-confidence is simple. It's a straightforward process, and if you use the content in this book and put it into practice, you will have a brand new outlook on life by the end of this course!

"Your relationship with yourself sets the tone for every other relationship you have." - Robert Holden

The Seven Steps to Finally Loving Yourself

INTRODUCTION

Hi there!

My name is Laurelle Burgham, but my friends call me Elle.

I'm a self-loving, enthusiastic woman who loves life and all it throws at me. I didn't use to be this way. In fact, 16 years ago, my life was less-than-amazing, but through the power of positive thinking and the right mental attitude, I've managed to turn that around completely, and I'm here to show you just how easy that can be.

I'm writing these words with the intention of sharing my personal wisdom with you. Some of it has been learned through a vast expanse of reading, and some of it has been passed down to me from my mentors in life. Now, I am passing it on to you with the hopes that it helps you create that AWESOME life you've always been dreaming of.

Just imagine it: a life where you're fulfilled, happy, a life where you love yourself. Love what you do. Love your friends and family members. Leading a life that's super rewarding and where you get to experience the best that this world has to offer!

I know Life can seem overbearing at times, but in retrospect, leading a great life where you have a deep love for yourself is not something that just happens by accident. It is a design and a constant effort.

I'll tell you all about my story - and the decision I made about how I wanted to live my life - in a bit.

For now, though, I want to tell you that I truly believe that happiness is something that can only exist when you start living life authentically, backed by your personal philosophy.

In life, my philosophy looks a little something like this:
- Life should be lived lovingly.
- Life, in essence, does not have restrictions. With the power of your mind, you have the ability to make and lift any restrictions and obstacles that stand in your way.
- Life should be lived in service of others. It keeps us humble and focused on the human experience.
- Life should be lived healthily. If our bodies are not healthy, there's no way our thoughts can be healthy.
- Life should be lived with the intent of learning something new every, single, day!

Why I Wrote This Book

I crafted my life, worked hard on my self-love, and continue to do so every day. Loving myself and my life is a given for me, but I also understand that the world out there can easily break people down, and the reality is that a lot of folks just don't know how to love themselves or what the amazing benefits of self-love are.

Childhood experiences, adverse influences from the media, materialism, and a general lack of interest grossly affect people, and if you don't keep tabs on yourself, it could very well spell your doom.

So I decided to write this book. Why? Because I felt like I had something to share with the world. I had found a recipe for success, and even more so, one that doesn't require years of practice and training, one that could help others regain their self-confidence and self-love with just a little tweak of their thoughts.

Yes, learning to love yourself and your life is hard work, but if you get it right the first time around, it's going to be one of the most rewarding investments you have ever made in yourself.

The words written in this book are meant to help you shift the way you see yourself and help you become a more awakened version of yourself. Essentially, the content in this book aims at rebuilding and strengthening the mind-body-soul connection you'll need to start loving yourself and embracing yourself for what you truly are. It strives to teach you about accepting who you are right now, at this moment, taking what you need from who you were yesterday, and building each and every day at who you want to be tomorrow.

Self-confidence and self-love is a practice. No two people on this earth are the same, yet we all have the same ticking parts, and if you understand how those parts work and are codependent on each other, you can begin to understand yourself better and the role you have in this life.

When it comes down to it, there's no ONE book that will give you definitive answers as to how you can go about rebuilding yourself and your self-confidence, but hopefully, with the mass of enlightening content you'll be reading through in this book, you'll have a comprehensive guide to rediscovering happiness, inevitably helping you learn to love yourself at the deepest level possible.

Who This Book Is For

This book will offer great value to all individuals out there looking for a way to rediscover happiness and love in their lives. Whether you're married with kids, or whether you're still studying and haven't even started thinking about what life after 25 will be like, this book is going to help you learn how to love yourself.

It'll teach you everything you need to know so that you'll be able to turn everyday, mundane situations, into incredible opportunities for living life to the fullest.

This book will benefit you if you're looking to gain absolute and irrepressible confidence in yourself. It will teach you how to have the confidence you need to free yourself from self-imposed limitations and fears that might be withholding you from a fantastic life. It will teach you about the importance of pursuing your dreams and living your life with purpose.

Not loving your self and being uncertain about yourself is a choice you make every day, it's about the behavioral patterns you choose to follow. It's about walking the walk and talking the talk. Loving yourself is a learned behavioral trait, and it's something that anyone can learn to do. As with all things in life, practice does make perfect, and if you follow my advice, you'll be living a loving life before you know it!

> *"One day I decided that I was beautiful, and so I carried out my life as if I was a beautiful girl. I wear colors that I really like, I wear makeup that makes me feel pretty, and it really helps. It doesn't have anything to do with how the world perceives you. What matters is what you see. Your body is your temple, it's your home, and you must decorate it." -Gabourey Sidibe*

How to Read This Book

As you're reading through this book, you'll see that I have a lot of information on how my life used to be, and what techniques I used to turn it around.

This book was not written with the intent of the reader simply copying and pasting the information into their diaries. The words in this book were written so that you can use them as a basis for writing your own philosophy. You can (and should) change and adapt my advice to make it your own, take what you can and learn from it before applying it to your own life.

If you're aiming at using the information in this book to its full potential, I'm going to have to ask you to step out of any traditional viewpoints you may have. Please enter a more conscious (relational) view before you read any further.

For the sake of digestibility, I've broken this book down into 11 chapters, and before you can move on to another one, you need to make sure you understand the content of each chapter and that you've taken some time to do each of the exercises mentioned in the content. You'll also notice that this book has been divided into two parts: Part One is where I'll tackle all the issues affecting self-love, and in Part Two, you can find all the solutions and ways in which you can start rebuilding your self-love.

With that said, let's kick things off and dive into my personal history, so that you can better understand my story and why there's so much method behind my madness!

In this book, you will learn the 7 secrets for loving yourself, which are:

- How to follow your life purpose and live an authentic life

- How cutting out media from your life can lead to self-love

- How to identify and eliminate limiting beliefs

- How advertising affects your self-love

- Why what you eat is what you are

- The importance of taking care of your mind, body and soul

- How meditation can help you unlock unconditional self-love

"Self-love is an ocean and your heart is a vessel. Make it full, and any excuses will spill over into the lives of people you hold dear. But you must come first." -Beau Tapin

CHAPTER 1

My Journey to Self-Love

If you're searching for that one person in the world that will make a dramatic and lasting change in your life, take a look in the mirror!

Over the course of 16 years, I have researched and studied what it takes to achieve total self-love and self-acceptance. It has been one of my greatest passions in life. I know, all too well, the pain that comes from living in the mental prison called "I'm not good enough". Having suffered from low self-esteem for more than a decade, I also understand how hard it can be to break free, step up to the plate, and start loving yourself unconditionally, without making any excuses for it.

You see, this is my story:

My childhood years were spent growing up in South Africa during the apartheid era. My mom and dad weren't lavishly rich, but we weren't suffering either. We lived a pretty middle-class life with just enough money for a few family vacations every year. Growing up wasn't hard work for my sister or me. We had everything we needed. Except the freedom to express ourselves, of course.

Our parents were strict. Mom definitely wore the pants in the house, and as the case with most other families of yesteryear was, in our house, kids were treated like kids: we weren't allowed to speak unless we were spoken to. We never butted into adult conversations, and if we even thought about back-chatting our parents, there would be hell to pay.

In retrospect, I wonder if their parenting approach was partly due to the fact that my mother was scared of what we would say, or perhaps it was because she was trying to be the perfect mother with the perfect kids that just smiled and nodded when they were spoken to. I never discussed it with my parents, but what I do know, is the fact that we didn't get to express ourselves, had an impact on me and my sister.

The way I was brought up had led to me becoming introverted, seriously lacking confidence, so much so that I didn't want to express my own thoughts and feelings in public. I remember a time where I was bullied at school for 12 months, stood up for myself but it never got better.

Things only got worse. Despite trying my best to find ways to make myself look 'pretty,' I always thought of myself as the runt of the pack. Friends were few and far between. The way I looked (*and how my body was changing throughout adolescence*) wasn't doing me any good either. Self-confidence self-love, and self-esteem were not words that existed in my mind and I suppose that's also part of the reason why my grades took a knock as well.

At one point, my mother enrolled me in a modelling program that lasted six months. The finishing school had taught me everything I needed to know about makeup, dressing for success, posture and how to captivate the audience with modelling competitions.

My modelling career was going great. For some reason, I was winning at this thing. I had taken home seven crowns in a very short period of time, and to this day, I still don't know how I pulled it off. I also bagged the title of 'Model of the Year' at my agency and it wasn't too long before I moved on to a bigger and better agency. I kept winning one competition after the other and time, and again, I was invited to do fashion shows for big brand names.

I was winning, but I definitely was not feeling victorious.

I was 13 years old when I met my to be first boyfriend. Like most other girls my age, I had been battling with acne, and just like most other girls, I resorted to makeup to help pretty up my appearance. I wanted to hide away under makeup. I tried everything to help clear up the problem, but regardless of how many different kinds of antibiotic creams, herbal teas, and skincare products I tried, nothing was working.

When I was 14 years old, a switch went on as far as my confidence levels were regarded. I won a beauty pageant called "Face of Miss Durban', which is a pretty big deal in the province I grew up in. I managed to take the crown home four times in a row. Suddenly people were calling me beautiful. I knew people were looking at me but did I feel like I was beautiful? Certainly not!

Even though I was taking home crowns and making serious progress with my modelling career, my childhood and the limiting beliefs I had of myself had gotten the better of me. At age 15, I still had only a few close friends, was starving myself to lose weight for upcoming modelling competitions, was still fighting the war against the acne that was taking over my face, and my self-confidence levels were at an all-time low.

When I turned 16 years old, my mother took me to see a Dermatologist. After a consultation and a serious chat about my skincare regime, the doctor prescribed Accutane. Accutane is a vitamin A skincare product that helps fight off excessive oil levels in the skin, plus it also promotes skin cell regeneration. Taking Accutane was something I'd always regret. The side-effects are terrible, and I'm still reaping the repercussions of using the product, to this day. I have dry skin and lips that peel weekly. These effects started the first week of using the product all those years ago. My lack of self-love was worsening. I never felt happy or content. I was always left hungering for something that I could feed my soul with, a purpose in life, a reason for me to love myself and my life.

And like a total accident, I stumbled upon Transcendental Meditation. I was actually introduced to the idea of TM by a friend, whose mother was a successful and well known TM teacher. She invited me to attend an introductory class. I was very dubious, but after reading up about it, I thought it might be beneficial in some way for me, and my dad pushed for me to pursue and learn the technique.

The introductory lesson had spiked an interest in me, which lead to me wanting to learn more about Transcendental Meditation.

The first time I meditated was quite an experience: after just 10 minutes of meditation, I was in a state of pure euphoric bliss, a feeling I had never experienced before. I felt like every fragment of stress in my body had lifted, and it had been replaced by soothing peace and relaxation.

Fast forward 16 years and I'm still practicing TM, 20 minutes in the morning, and again 20 minutes each night before I head off to bed. For me, the practice has brought me into complete balance with myself and my surroundings and helped me on my journey to self-love.

I have studied and researched the effects of meditation and a positive mindset, and I have concluded that anyone can use the techniques I mention in this book to rediscover self-love. I hope that you'll take the information I'm about to give you and use it to boost your self-confidence. I want to help you create a joyful life experience where everything just flows. It's time to let go of your innate fears, those self-imposed limitations.

It's time for you to start pursuing your dreams, start living your purpose, and start making a difference in the world. As you go through this journey of self-discovery, it is my hope that you understand that self-love and self-confidence must be part of who you are. It shouldn't be just a behavior, but a way of life.

"Self-love is so important. Loving anything is impossible until you fall in love with who you are. As humans, we are always changing, always growing, always taking two steps forward and one step back, but during the ups and the downs, who's there? No one but you can pick yourself up when you're feeling down. No one can make you happier than you can make yourself if you allow it. Nothing can bring you down unless you let it. Loving who you are and embracing who you are going to become in the next minute, hour, day, week, month, year, etc. is only going to make you happier. You're going to radiate positivity because you love who you are. There is nothing better than that and once you experience it, let me tell you, you'll understand why. LOVE YOURSELF. I will never ever stop saying it, putting emphasis on it, and working for it." -Unknown

The Seven Steps to Finally Loving Yourself

CHAPTER 2

The Meaning and Importance of Self-Esteem

Self-love and self-esteem is the way you *feel* about yourself. It's about the **worth** you place on yourself. It's the level of competence you believe you possess to do things successfully in life. When you respect and believe in yourself as a worthy person, you acknowledge your personal strengths and weaknesses as a human being.

One of the single most important factors for experiencing joy, happiness, and overall success in life is ACCEPTING WHO YOU ARE, loving yourself for all that you are. Once you understand the importance of truthfully and unconditionally loving yourself and your life, you'll discover just how incredible this journey called *life* can really be.

When you have great self-esteem, you'll be able to determine your standards for what you are willing to accept or settle for in life.

Self-esteem also helps determine just how well you take care of your physical and mental health, what you feel you're able to achieve in life, the way in which other people treat you, and even whether or not other people feel inclined to be around you.

Why is this? Well, it's because when you're confident in yourself when you've got great self-esteem, you'll radiate positive energy. You'll make other people feel safe in your presence. When you are confident in yourself, you have a sense of certainty within yourself that you're willing and able to tackle any obstacle that life gives you.

Having great self-esteem means never asking yourself:
Can I really do this?
What if this backfires on me?
Am I even good enough to pull this off?

When you have great self-esteem, it means that once you have a goal in mind, you **believe** that it will happen. You accept the fact that certain goals take some time to work on, but you never doubt in your own abilities to achieve them.

The Difference between Self-Love and Self-Esteem

Self-love and self-esteem are not one in the same thing, although a lot of people believe that idea. The fact that they support each other cannot be denied, but at their core, they are two different things.

Self-love and self-esteem are built from a set of similar factors, but they are different aspects of the way you see yourself and the way you treat yourself.

When you have self-esteem, you can build self-love, and when you have self-love, it becomes easier to build self-esteem.

To me, great self-esteem comes from being proud of who and what you are, of what you can do. It might be related to just one aspect of who you are. Self-love is an overall self-acceptance of who you are as a person, despite your flaws, which creates an inner desire to take good care of yourself and focus on what truly makes you happy in life.

I want you to understand those elemental differences, so you don't short-change yourself by mistaking self-esteem for self-love. I believe that while you can have good and healthy self-esteem without totally loving yourself for who you are, self-love is usually accompanied by good self-esteem. I've met a lot of people who were super confident in one area of their lives and thought that was the route to self-love. But they didn't treat themselves lovingly, which is why they were never able to achieve deep self-love.

From my experiences, having self-love is more prevalent than loving yourself deeply and unconditionally. It's being able to have good self-esteem in all areas of your life.

You might be super confident about your job, but not necessarily about the skills you have.

Or you might attract people into your life with your great looks, but you don't feel smart, or skillful, or like you deserve those people in your life for reasons other than your looks.

You might feel amazing working a computer job, but when it comes to real life, you're less than confident. Or you might be an excellent communicator with people whom you know and trust, but as soon as you're exposed to a group of people in public, you suddenly freeze up.

When you love yourself deeply, you accept yourself with all of your shortcomings, and your self-love improves your overall self-esteem.

After years of being down in the dumps, I decided that the only way out of it was by starting to love myself again. I looked for special aspects of myself, and even though I was still insecure about a lot of aspects about myself, I started to fall in love with myself again.

I started feeling good about my accomplishments in life, and I started to realize that no matter where I am or who I'm with, I'm a successful woman with great self-esteem about my abilities in life.

The truth is that good self-esteem in one area can turn into cockiness or conceit, which is not loving behavior towards yourself. It's great to think well of yourself, but not to a point where you think you're better than other people among you.

Good self-esteem is feeling good about you in positive (not arrogant) ways. An arrogant attitude often occurs when you don't love yourself deeply and you're motivated by your insecurities, flaunting what you have to make up for what you don't. People who have true self-esteem treat others well, and the same goes for people that truly love themselves.

When you start integrating the confidence from the self-esteem you may have in one area of your life, it can blossom into a strong self-love. Make sure you pay attention to how you feel in different situations.

Notice when you feel the most confident and then remind yourself that you're the same person in all other areas of your life.

Love all of it - the very good way you handle yourself sometimes - and the time you're not as great as you'd like to be.

None of us are perfect, and you know what? That's okay. As long as you can accept that and keep in mind that we're all perfectly imperfect, you've got the key to a winning recipe.

True self-esteem and self-love include self-acceptance, as you are right now. When you are able to accept who and what you are - including your shortcomings - you can have good self-esteem and a strong sense of self-love.

The Importance of Self-Esteem

When you love yourself and have great self-esteem, it means that:
- You're more likely to value your health and your body
- You're more likely to earn more since you recognize your true value and worth
- You're more likely to have successful relationships, whether they're romantic or just friendships.

People with good self-esteem find it easy to establish stable relationships. Only when you love yourself can you truly love someone else. People are much more likely to recognize the value in you if *you* see the value in you.

Also, because you value yourself too much to accept anything less than a loving relationship, you don't punish yourself or self-sabotage anymore by entering negative relationships.

People with healthy self-esteem manage their lives much better. Their lives are usually free from stress, worries, and constraint, and they enjoy ease, relaxation and the feeling of self-satisfaction.

Loving yourself strengthens everything in you. It strengthens your auric field around you, which is your first line of defense. Conversely, doubting yourself, criticizing yourself, hating yourself, judging yourself, bad-mouthing yourself, and belittling yourself weakens you.

When we are born, we're all completely fearless; we feel no pressure to conform.

Have you noticed how self-confident kids are? It's because they're empowered, and they either do what they enjoy doing, or they don't participate at all. What an amazing concept!

When we're kids, we live in the 'here and now.' We live in constant wonder and amazement, and we're willing to explore anything and everything, and we have no fear of the unknown.

Then we mature a little, and we're exposed to the fears of our parents, which are totally unauthentic. Outside of our minds, those fears simply do not exist.

So here's my question: Just imagine what would happen if you were to adopt a child-like belief in yourself?

As adults, most of us don't try new things because we're afraid of failure, but imagine a baby failing at walking and then deciding never to try it again.

The fears we have, the broken down self-love and self-esteem, all of that is based on learned behavior, illusions that exist nowhere other than in our minds.

What Causes Low Self-Esteem?

The simple answer to the question is that people *make* that decision. They *decide* that they aren't good enough, that they can't do it, or that there's something wrong with them.

Take a child whose parents lack self-esteem: It's almost guaranteed that the kid will grow up with the exact same behavior he <u>learned</u> from his parents. In most cases, low self-esteem is caused by monkey see, monkey do.

When it comes to shaping human character, a child's family life and his upbringing have a massive impact on his self-esteem, and I believe that being able to express yourself as a child, whenever the need arises, should never be underestimated.

As kids, we are open to everything that happens, and we don't have control over much of what we hear, see or experience. Experiences we have when growing up - and our relationships with family members - can impact our self-esteem. For example:

- Being severely disciplined
- Being screamed at and ordered around
- Being disregarded
- Being belittled and told you're doing everything wrong
- Being given high but impossible expectations
- Being told that fortune or luck produces results, so helplessness is the outcome
- Being told that if you fail, you're no good
- Being compared unfavorably to siblings or other children
- Being neglected

Conversely, positive and loving parenting develops healthy confidence and self-esteem.

- Receiving kisses and hugs
- Being spoken to in a polite manner
- Being listened to
- Being praised
- Being given high and achievable expectations
- Being told that effort over time produces results, so obstacles are accepted
- Being told that failure happens to everyone, so disappointments are accepted
- Being valued for who you are
- Receiving attention and care

Self-Love Influencers during the Age of Adolescence

Adolescence and the years we spend at school massively impact our self-love, whether we want to admit it or not. Young individuals face many challenges that impact and negatively affect their self-confidence, self-esteem, and self-love from the time they turn 13 up until they reach the age of 18.

Not only do we go from being kids to young adults, but during adolescence, we also have to deal with a hot mess of physical and emotional changes in our lives. Feelings of inadequacy, loneliness, the abuse of substances, a tendency to avoid reality, and self-destructive behavior are common in kids that have diminished self-love during adolescence.

Teenagers are given the world to explore, but the world is also expecting big things from them. There's pressure from friends and family. There's pressure from school. There's pressure from boyfriends and girlfriends. It's all a scary mess.

They're being compared and comparing themselves to others.

They're always trying to get their grades up.

They're obsessed about what boys or girls think of them.

Girls fret over the fact that they might not be pretty enough.

They're obsessing over their bodies.

Their hormones are going crazy, they're going through puberty and the peer pressure is worse now than it was a decade ago, and it'll only get worse as time passes.

The truth is that during adolescence, self-love is influenced by an array of external factors, but kids that have healthy self-esteem tend to:
- Make friends with ease
- Get accepted into group settings easily
- Have no problems with bullying
- Have great grades
- Sleep well
- Be motivated to study and do well at school
- Be happy
- Get along great with their peers
- Have healthy eating habits
- Have positive energy levels

On the other hand, adolescents that have low self-esteem tend to:
- Get sick easily so they don't have to go to school
- Not get accepted by social groups
- Be bullied
- Be unhappy
- Have low grades
- Get into trouble on a constant basis
- Have little or no motivation in life
- Have a serious lack of energy
- Eat very poorly
- Be surrounded by a negative energy

Why is Self-Esteem and Positive Body Image So Important during Adolescence?

Self-esteem is all about how much you feel you are worth — and how much you feel other people value you. Self-esteem is important because feeling good about yourself can affect your mental health and how you behave, and ultimately your self-love.

People with high self-esteem know themselves well. They're realistic and find friends that like and appreciate them for who they are. People with high self-esteem usually feel more in control of their lives and know their own strengths and weaknesses.

Body image is how you view your physical self — including whether you feel you are attractive and whether others like your looks. For many people, especially people in their early teens, body image can be closely linked to self-esteem.

What Influences a Person's Self-Esteem During the Teenage Years?

Puberty and Development
Some people struggle with their self-esteem and body image during puberty because it's a time when the body goes through many changes. These changes, combined with wanting to feel accepted by our friends, means it can be tempting to compare ourselves with others. The trouble with that is, not everyone grows or develops at the same pace.

Media (a.k.a. the devil)
During our early teens, we become more aware of celebrities and media images — as well as how other kids look and how we fit in. We might start to compare ourselves with other people or media images ("ideals" that are frequently airbrushed). All of this can affect how we feel about ourselves and our bodies even as we grow into our teens.

Self-Image

Our self-image is how we see ourselves, not how we think others see us, in terms of our own abilities, physical appearance, and personality.

Our past conditioning and experiences make up our self-image as it is today.

Our self-image determines the outcome of what we do. If it's positive, we're optimistic and surrounded by good energy. If it's negative, well, negative thoughts fill our minds.

Our self-image either causes us to lead a happy and successful life or a miserable life, in which we believe we are inadequate, lacking in intelligence and incompetence.

We need to understand that our self-image accepts whatever is put into it. It does not differentiate good stuff from bad stuff that goes into it.

External sources play a part in the creation of our poor self-image. This comes from an accumulation of bad experiences or nasty remarks from other people.

Self-image is also affected by other people's attitudes towards us.

Many people, not all, who are handicapped suffer from lasting poor self-image. They feel hopeless and helpless and experience low levels of self-worth, self-confidence and self-esteem.

But that's only half the story.

In some cases, low self-esteem can also be caused by being reprimanded for making mistakes. As kids, we have SO MANY opportunities to fail at things so that we have the opportunity of eventually getting them right. And that's how we learn. We learn with trial and error.

A lot of us are afraid to try new things because we have an inherent fear of failure. We love our comfort zones, and we'll stay there just for the sake of avoiding failure. We're also scared of rejection, which has a lot of us focusing on the thoughts of others. We fear that if we don't do or say the right things, other people will disapprove. As a result, we start living lives far below our potential.

Our need for love, connection, and acceptance from others is one of the most powerful influencers in our lives; it might even be the reason behind why we *do* most of what we do in life.

Then there's also the case of the media. At its best, the media is a bad influence, and you can probably guess what the worst form here is. Why? Because they feed us a picture of how we *ought* to be.

We crumble under peer pressure because we just want to *fit in* with the crowd. Before you know it, you're not **feeling** rich enough, smart enough, pretty enough, fit enough, skinny enough, and you don't have a relationship that fits the 'mold'.

But here's the funny thing: 99% of people out there are terrified of what YOU think of them. Just some food for thought!

Signs of Low Self-Esteem
- Inauthentic, pretentious, and fearful behavior
- Trying to find justifications for all of your actions
- Always trying to place the blame on other people
- Seeing yourself as a victim
- Making up invalid reasons for why nothing in your life seems to work out
- Exaggeration, manipulation, and lying
- Attention-seeking
- Unable to say no and stand up for what you believe in
- Blaming other people for your problems
- Resentment and hate
- Guilt and shame for one's actions
- Procrastination, stress, and worry

- Loneliness
- Depression

Signs of High Self-Esteem
- Taking responsibility for your own life and results
- Being a leader
- Taking a stand for what you believe in
- Courage, truthfulness, and integrity
- Pursuing your dreams and being an inspiration to others
- Creativity, patience, and perseverance
- Taking action on your ideas
- Being free from the need for approval from others
- Being grateful, optimistic, loving life, and being solution-oriented
- Living life in the here and now
- Having pride and honor
- Exhibiting a passion for life and an overall good energy
- Forgiveness and letting go of the past
- Being committed, passionate, and enthusiastic about life and all its possibilities

Understanding Emotions and How They Impact Self-Love

Emotions and emotional triggers provide us with opportunities for growth, where we get to know ourselves a little better. They're also there to allow us to consciously decide who it is we want to be and how we want to show up in the world. Your level of self-confidence depends largely on how well you choose to express yourself.

Every day, we're all faced with an abundance of emotional triggers, and they're all there to test our ability to manage our emotions and our behavior. The important thing, however, is being mindful of long-lasting, provoking triggers that can fuel discord in our daily lives.

Understanding Emotional Triggers

Emotional triggers present themselves in the form of people or events that set off intense emotional reactions within us, and dealing with this (in the right way) is essential to your personal development and your self-love.

When we don't appropriately manage our emotional triggers, they can cause a lack of self-love, lead to acute distress, and cause interpersonal conflict. They can also become a roadblock between the personal success you want and need to achieve in life.

Frustration, fear, anger, insecurity, defensiveness and jealousy are just some of the emotions that are activated by emotional triggers. They can also lead to emotional outbursts, which might force us to develop a set of coping mechanisms which will only lead to more internal conflict.

The truth is that emotional triggers serve as mirrors for our own intentions, and when handled correctly, can provide us with a better way of seeing ourselves.

Emotional triggers reflect a threat to your identity, which ultimately affects your behavior. At first, you might be triggered by an event or merely seeing a certain person, but the real threat, however, is what that person or that event symbolizes that threatens your worldview or your sense of security.

Emotional triggers have a lot less to do with how we feel about some people or some events and actually have a lot MORE to do with your own values, your own judgments, and how you view yourself. More often than not, emotional triggers present themselves whenever our wounded or challenged egos are at play.

How Thought Influences Emotional Triggers

Our external environments, as well as our internal experiences, can have an impact on whether or not we fall victim to emotional triggers, and thoughts about the past, the present, and the future have a massive impact on emotional triggers.

Thoughts about the actions of others are a major cause of emotional triggers. You might be thinking about why someone would want to do something you'd never dream of doing, which could easily lead to rage and anger.

Your emotional triggers can also be caused by primary emotions. Let's say that in the past, you've felt scared by someone's anger. Becoming angry yourself might then cause you to feel fearful. Your anger scared you so much because it had reminded you of a past incident. But just because you feel it doesn't necessarily mean it's true, in fact, it rarely turns out that way.

Getting Over Emotional Triggers
Our brains, as you might know, have no way of discriminating between perceived reality and imaginary reality. It doesn't know the difference between a real situation and a very strong emotion that's just coming through. This is why it's imperative to learn how to manage thoughts and unjustified emotions so that you can decrease your stress levels and the effect they have on your body.

You have to start by identifying the trigger. Once you've pointed out the culprit, it gives your rational mind the opportunity of managing the emotion.

Next, you have to remember that thoughts are just that - thoughts. Sometimes our thoughts are seriously inaccurate. Sometimes they're not true, and there's no way of knowing what the truth is until we have all the facts, the evidence. Make sure you look for evidence or proof before you mindlessly accept your thoughts as true and correct.

Just because you're feeling something, it doesn't necessarily make it true. It's just like with the fake thoughts thing. Feelings can also be wrong or untrue. Make sure you're looking for evidence that your thoughts and your feelings are valid and true before you act on them.

The last weapon you'll need for getting rid of emotional triggers is staying mindful. Stay in the present and don't dwell on the past or fret about what the future might hold. Right there, right now, that's where your thoughts, your feelings, and your mindset needs to be. It's the only way to ensure you're feeling authentic emotions, that you perceive the situation with a clear mind, and that you're not allowing your self-esteem to be broken down by disillusioned ideas or misconceptions.

Exercise

The first step you're going to have to take toward regaining your self-love and building your self-esteem is to go out and buy a journal, funny as it might sound. With the help of your journal, you're going to figure out WHO you are and WHAT your life's purpose is. You'll be using your journal to analyze your behavioural traits and also using that information to find ways in which you can regain happiness in your life.

Essentially, you'll be using your journal to write down all the aspects of your life that you'd like to change, everything you no longer want to be written as part of your life's story, and also, you'll be writing down your new life story.

When you read through your journal at the end of this book, you'll realize that everything you are is essentially a result of what you have thought. You'll realize that the fears and beliefs you have in your life limit your true self, and you'll see that those fears are not only illogical, but they are also disempowering.

So here's your first exercise: When you're in a mood that allows you to be totally honest with yourself, write down the answers to these questions:
- What do you remember about your family life, growing up, that helped you develop healthy self-esteem?
- What do you remember about your family life, growing up, that led to low self-esteem and self-love?
- What are you not happy about in your life at the moment? Is there anything you can do to change the situation?

- What is the one reality about yourself that is difficult to accept?
- When do you feel most frustrated with yourself?
- What are the five fears that you currently have? What do you fear most in your life right now? Why? What would happen if these fears became a reality?
- Complete the following sentences:
- *I like myself least when I...*
- *I love myself most when I...*

CHAPTER 3

How Self-Love Affects Your Life

When I was growing up, I was constantly reminded about the importance of going to school, getting a degree, and then getting a decent job. Most folks know the feeling all too well. We live paycheque to paycheque just to survive, and before we know it, we're living on credit because we simply can't afford to keep up with the Jones'.

I have found that net worth equals self-worth. Why? Because people that have a lot of self-love tend to approach life and work differently. They don't live just to work.

Most of us have fallen victim to the "I'm not good enough" trap, whether it's in our professional lives or our relationships. We become determined to fake it until we make it. We cover up our "not good enough" issues, and we hope and pray nobody discovers our flaws.

But it's absurd really.

Many people out there work very hard to achieve success, only to come to the conclusion that they still feel inadequate, almost like underneath all of their achievements, they stand as impostors. Success keeps the wolf away from the door for a maximum of 30 seconds.

The truth is that achieving 'success' as the world out there defines it, will never fulfill you. You'll arrive at the end of your life and get a "Wow, you've worked so hard, and you've suffered through it all. You led such an honorable life…" and then BOOM, you're dead.

Trying to look good, striving to be on top of your game and faking self-esteem is utterly inauthentic, and it's out of integrity with the true self and your life's goal.

The truth behind being successful in life is simple: You have to discover your passion and then start LIVING it! If it fills you up with joy, it's not hard work; you're going to be joyous and present at the moment, while also making a decent living.

WHAT you think about relationships is the first and most important factor in establishing and maintaining a healthy relationship. Your beliefs DO NOT impact the real truth, but they do impact YOU. Your beliefs rule your behavior, which is why it's imperative to identify limiting beliefs and either change or get rid of them altogether.

You see, when your self-esteem is not where it ought to be, it's easy to fall victim to negative self-talk and limiting beliefs.

Limiting beliefs are formed out of low self-worth and zero self-love.

Here are some common limiting beliefs that people with low self-esteem have:
- If I've fallen out of love with my partner, I can't get it back
- My past experiences are bound to become my future experiences
- To make anything in life work, my circumstances have to change
- If only 'this' would happen, the world would be a better place
- I don't have the power in me to change my situation

How Self-Esteem Affects Your Productivity

A lot of people think that low self-esteem means it only has a detrimental effect on our goals, but usually, we think about how low self-esteem causes us to avoid starting something or quit before achieving success. We don't think about our day-to-day actions that can be affected by low self-esteem, like our jobs and our performance.

Whether you're a solo-flyer and have you're own business or personal projects you're working on, or you're an employee in a large company, or even an entrepreneur with your own small company, the only way you'll achieve success is by taking action towards your goal. That action has to have quantity and quality. But if you suffer from low self-esteem, you could unwittingly be sabotaging your best efforts.

Here's how: You might have noticed how some people at work seem to be very skilled and wise in their area of expertise, but their performance and their output aren't quite on-par, and almost falls short of their potential and their abilities. Their performance just doesn't match their potential.

The reason for this is because they do NOT believe in themselves, they allow themselves to do less than they're capable of because they're scared of the outcomes if they challenge themselves. In some cases, they believe in their own abilities, but they just don't feel worthy of success, so they never even bother trying in the first place.

We can define self-esteem as *"the experience of being capable of meeting life's challenges and being worthy of happiness,"* as quoted by the National Association for Self-Esteem.

When people lack self-esteem, they don't believe that they're capable or worthy of great results, and even though their skills and knowledge may be more than adequate, they never try what they actually know they'll be able to achieve.

Furthermore, people that lack self-esteem don't believe they're worthy of great results and so they unconsciously "dumb down" their work as to not stand out, not be noticed, or outperform their peers.

Low self-esteem causes an abundance of issues in the workplace. If you have a poor perception of your competencies and your abilities, you'll feel like you don't deserve success, you might be programming yourself for failure, or, at best, mediocrity.

In essence, your efforts and the results you achieve at work will just never be able to measure up to your true potential.

When it comes to a lack of belief in capability and lack of belief in worthiness, there's a **very important aspect at play**. Those who believe they're competent but unworthy tend to become more boastful. This then backfires when their true accomplishments don't measure up to their claims.

Then there are people who truly think that they're worthy, but are incompetent, those people tend to blame others and their circumstances for the lack of results, but they never blame themselves.

So, how can you raise your competency and your belief in your own worth, so that you're able to excel in your career and become more productive in any endeavor you choose to take on?

You make a deal with yourself.

You promise yourself that for 1% of every day - *which comes down to two minutes a day* - you'll avoid doing anything that makes you feel bad about yourself, and instead, you'll focus on doing something that's empowering and that makes you feel good about yourself!

Instead of talking to your best friend about how you never come in line for a promotion at work, try talking to your friend about how grateful you are for your job and what you're learning on a daily basis.

Instead of lighting up that damaging cigarette, you'll endeavor to sit down for two minutes, do some breathing exercises, and become more aware of where you are and what you're doing.

Instead of blaming a co-worker for a failed project, you'll brainstorm a few ways in which you can better work together as a team and achieve success for the higher good.

Instead of frowning, you'll focus on spending two minutes a day smiling.

Instead of blaming others, you'll find ways in which you can complement others at the office.

Instead of worrying about deadlines and projects, you'll find time to meditate on a daily basis.

Instead of putting yourself down for the things you were not able to achieve today, you'll find new ways of complementing yourself and highlighting your amazing capabilities.

Instead of giving in to fear, you'll find ways to encourage yourself instead.

Instead of focusing on the worst possible outcome, you'll endeavor to envision the best outcome for the scenario.

Tuning into a better state of mind will take some time, but when it does, that one percent of positivity on a daily basis will make a difference in your life and will help boost your self-esteem, which ultimately helps increase your productivity at work.

How Your Past Affects Your Present

The way you're feeling right now, the personality traits you have and the behaviour you're using from one day to another were all shaped by past events that you went through.

Experiences you had as a kid still have the power to impact your life at present, even the smallest of experiences that might seem insignificant and irrelevant.

Right at the very core of your belief system, you'll find the memories of early childhood that shaped your views of the world. This is why so many adults today still carry around limiting beliefs that were formed in their childhood years.

But here's a little-known secret: You CAN stop your past from affecting the present!
How? You start becoming aware of the most significant and influential childhood experiences that shaped the person you are today. If they're easy to recall, those memories are probably the ones that had the biggest impact on your life.

Exercise

Now that you understand how self-love and self-esteem affect your work life and your relationships, and how old memories from the past can influence your present day life, it's time you started creating some positive affirmations for yourself.

Feel free to write down the following affirmations on a vision board, somewhere you'll be able to see them every single day. Use them, make them your own, and then say them to yourself on a daily basis until you start making them part of your internal dialogue...

1. I CAN fall in love again. I CAN clear the obstacles that stand between me and true love.
2. I CAN find my passion and live it. I do NOT have to slave away for a job I hate.
3. I CAN create new experiences.
4. I take full responsibility for the quality of my professional career and my relationships.
5. My past does NOT equal my future.
6. The quality of my life is NOT dictated by my circumstances, but rather by my reactions to them.
7. I am powerful and have the ability to change and enjoy my life.
8. Love is unlimited, and as long as I love myself and life, I will never be without love

"No matter how many times you tell a girl she is beautiful, she will never believe you if she doesn't believe in herself." - Unknown

CHAPTER 4

Fear - And How to Overcome It

There's nothing that can repress human potential and diminish energy levels quite like living in constant fear and with worry. In order to regain your energy levels, and get to a place where you're ready to fall in love with yourself again, you need to demonstrate the courage to face your fears.

Remember this: It doesn't really matter what ANYONE else thinks. You DON'T need to win anybody's approval. This is your life, and these are YOUR dreams, and you get to lead your life on your own terms.

So how do we dissolve fear? We start with love.

Neale Donald Walsch said: "All human actions are motivated at their deepest level by one of two emotions – love or fear. Fear is the energy which contracts, closes down, draws in, runs, hides, hoards, harms. Love is the energy which expands, opens up, sends out, stays, reveals, shares, heals."

I speak from experience, and I can tell you that I spent most of my life being fearful. I was scared and fearful of pretty much everything. Fear of rejection. Fear of not being perfect enough. Fear of not fitting in. Fear of not fitting the mold that society had set in place for me.

The problem is that fear is an element that exists in our **minds**, and when we feed it instead of fighting it, it can start controlling us.

Through the help of daily affirmations, consistent practice of self-love, and daily exercises, I've managed to take control and conquer my fears. It's amazing to note that once the fear is gone, the world becomes your oyster.

I'll tell you this: It is only once you start fighting your fears that you'll be able to get rid of the barrier that's keeping you from excelling in life.

Although I learn something new every day, it is through my experiences that I have learned:

- Fear is an unpleasant emotion or thought.
- Fear is that feeling you get when you are afraid or worried that something bad is about to happen.
- As far as human progress is concerned, the feeling of fear has to be one of the greatest impediments.
- Our innate human nature dictates that we'll all feel fear at one stage or another during our lives, but the key to controlling it (and not letting it control you) is not empowering it so that it never has the opportunity to adversely influence your actions or your decisions.
- If you feel like your confidence is undermined and like any real chances of success you have in this life are being compromised, that's fear talking.
- Fear can be an imaginary aspect of your mind, or it can be a real threat in your everyday existence, and you experience fear because you have a misperception or misjudgment of a situation.
- When you're feeling anxious, insecure, and completely lacking in positivity, that's fear talking. When you're fearful, you have a growing tendency to become hesitant about new opportunities in life, and you're also more likely to procrastinate. All logical

thoughts and reasoning abilities tend to fly out the window when fear kicks in.
- Fear is what's standing between you and your true potential and all the possibilities in your life. If you don't control your fears, it can easily ruin perfectly great relationships you have with others.
- Countless negative thoughts fuel fear. If you're fearful of disease, old age, loneliness, victimization, ridicule, poverty, death, an accident, ghosts…that's fear talking, and the more you fear these things, the more control the fear has over you.
- When you can directly confront your fears, they'll start to wither away and eventually die off.
- Once you start filling your mind with courageous thoughts, there's no more room for fears, which leads to you making more courageous decisions in life.
- There's only one thing standing between you and your dreams: Fear.

All that exists in your life, whether it's good or bad, is there because of your beliefs, your thoughts, your choices, your actions, and your attitude.

You, and you alone have manifested these situations in your life, you've attracted situations and people into your life through your way of being and through your thoughts.

Just like happiness, joy, sadness and anger, fear is an emotion, and the best way to overcome it and get rid of it is to own up to it.

The Limitations You Create for Self-Love

Think about your life right now.

Are you living the kind of life you think you should be living?

Do you have everything that you'd like to have in life?

Are you where you want and need to be in life right now?

If you couldn't answer those questions with a positive YES, then you're likely limiting your abilities with limited thinking, with negative self-talk, without self-love and with your limiting beliefs.

Before you can decide what it is you'd *like* to achieve with your life - whether it's for the sake of yourself, your family, or your business - you need to **sort out your priorities**. One of the most urgent priorities is to start believing in yourself, that you are MORE capable of achieving all that you set out to do than you ever imagined.

The only limitations on what you can *(or can't)* achieve are your thoughts. Your limited thinking is largely the result of your false beliefs. Your beliefs, whether they're limiting or empowering, were formed through your experiences, perceptions, and assumptions of life.

Limiting beliefs are assumptions you made about reality that simply isn't true, and when we want our actions to have a positive effect on our lives, our beliefs need to be as close to reality as possible.

Fundamentally, human perception and reality are two different things, so while the presence of some kind of limiting belief will always be there, we can begin closing the gap between reality and our perception thereof with the help of observation and openness to new information.

So what is observation?

It is a required state of mind we need to find new ideas and habits. Marcus Aurelius said: "Observe always that everything is the result of a change, and get used to thinking that there is nothing Nature loves so well as to change existing forms and to make new ones like them."

Observations point us in the right direction and show us how to observe reality, instead of just sitting back and believing what everyone else is saying about it.
When we mindfully observe our surroundings, we're able to determine how our assumptions might be distorting our perceptions of reality,

and we get a better idea of what internal beliefs have to change before we can evolve into the most content versions of ourselves.

Being **open to new information** is yet another aspect of changing limiting beliefs in order to regain our self-love.

You see, when we use the experiences and beliefs of others to test our own, we're almost taking a shortcut towards finding and eliminating our limiting beliefs.

When we're open to new information, we're adopting an enabling belief. Not only does being open to new ideas imply being open to using new solutions to old problems, but it also involves trying out ideas you never liked at all. When we cultivate curiosity in both ideas that sound amazing and the ones we absolutely loathe, we're open to new ideas, and we're getting rid of our limiting beliefs.

Do NOT take these words as a means to blindly accept every idea that this world has on offer though. You're NOT practicing stupidity here, but instead, you're objectively *entertaining the idea*, seeing if it's able to add any meaning to your life, and then deciding whether or not you'll use or lose it.

Whether you'd like to admit it or not, your limiting beliefs, the ones that are blocking your road towards self-love, they are all conditioned perceptions that were built up on memories of pain and pleasure.

It's true that the assumptions we make about life and the people we share it with are what help us make better sense of our world; so in essence, we use our beliefs as anchors that help express our understanding of our world.

It's in our *human nature* to tend to cling to our beliefs, regardless of whether or not they're serving us in the present moment. Why? Because our beliefs help us feel **safe** and **secure**, which all comes back to the basic human need for **certainty**, which is something we all crave.

When you become stuck in the present moment, unable to move forward with your life, it's probably because you might still be holding on to beliefs that served you earlier on in life but have no real purpose for you at the moment. Instead of helping you feel safe and secure, those limiting beliefs are keeping you captive because they simply aren't compatible with your lifestyle anymore.

Your **beliefs lie at the very core of who you are**, and they impact every aspect of your life, in every conceivable way. Our beliefs impact our intelligence and our decision making. They determine our self-talk and self-analysis.

Our beliefs influence our ability to think creatively, constructively, and critically. Your beliefs massively impact your self-esteem and how you feel about your life in general.

Your beliefs are either pushing you to go out and do something, or they're forcing you to watch the opportunity pass by. They determine which goals you set for yourself, and they also determine your methodology for achieving those goals.

All of this comes down to one simple thing: If you don't have your beliefs aligned with your goals and objectives for your life, you're going to find it hard to practice self-love, and you're going to be left feeling miserable and unfulfilled.

Sowing and Reaping

The universal law of sowing and reaping is the same as the law of cause and effect.

The law says that there's an output to every input.

It states that what you are reaping today is a result of what you have sowed in the past. What you are experiencing now is the sweet or bitter fruit of whatever actions you had taken or decisions you made during the course of your life.
The law of sowing and reaping has governed human destiny since the beginning of time.

Every member of the human species is subjected to it.

No one can claim they are free from its control. Whether you enjoy success or happiness, or failure or distress, it is due solely to how you have acted, whether in compliance with or in violation of the law.

When you are successful or happy, others say you are lucky, which is not the case.

The law favors no being. It's fair and impartial.

Those who are successful have put in much effort to attain their successful status.

They work hard and do many different things to increase their probabilities to be successful and eventually they are. Others, who are less successful or have failed, lay the blame on their luck.

The successful ones reap what they sow while the unsuccessful ones fail to reap what they do not sow.

This law is all about a perfect balance of cause and reaction. You get no reaction when you don't act.

There are people who believe they can get something out of nothing. When the law of sowing and reaping applies, they certainly get nothing. There are others who believe in shortcut to success and riches. They make attempts to be successful or get rich quickly without putting in much effort.
Even if they succeed, their successes and riches will not last. But mostly, they get nothing out of nothing, or they learn the hard way that there is no shortcut to their desired goals as long as they act in violation of the law.

You are responsible for yourself and whatever you do.
If your outer world is making you feel unfulfilled, the power lies in your hands to change it, starting with your inner world.

Let's take an example: You want people to stop ignoring you. Now, we all have an instinctive need to feel accepted by others, so this could be a major deal. The first step you'd take towards tackling the situation would be to not ignore other people, and instead have a friendly demeanor. You give a little; you get a lot. It's a simple rule that still rings true to this day.

What you experience - *whether it is good or bad* - is the effect of your deeds. As a human being, you're being held liable for your actions by the law of reaping and sowing. The way you act will inevitably depend on your beliefs, and if you have limiting beliefs, you need to work on clearing them out of your mind and your life for good.

Exercise

Taking everything I've just mentioned into consideration, I want you to write down all the limiting beliefs that come to mind when you think about your goals of achieving self-love and healthy self-esteem. In your journal, write down the answers to these questions:

1. What kind of resistance do you feel inside of you when you think about improving your level of self-love?
2. What challenges hold me back from achieving that goal?
3. What excuses do you tend to indulge in when it comes to this goal?
4. Why do you make those excuses?
5. Why do you think that the goal is too hard to achieve?
6. What do you tend to blame others for?
7. Do you think that you could have psychological rules that are preventing you from moving forward in life?
8. Are the standards you've set for yourself in life too low?
9. Are your core values in conflict with your goal of achieving self-love?
10. As you're working towards your goal, how are you labeling yourself?
11. Do you have any specific rules about what you should or shouldn't do or what should or shouldn't happen in your life?

Having answered those questions, it's time to sit down and find out what limiting beliefs are holding you back. Write down the answers to these questions:

1. What beliefs are holding you back in life?
2. How are those beliefs preventing you from reaching your goals?
3. How are those beliefs denying you the opportunity of becoming the person you want to be?

"If only you could sense how important you are to the lives of those you meet; how important you can be to people you may never even dream of. There is something of yourself that you leave at every meeting with another person."
– Fred Rogers

CHAPTER 5

The Self-Love, Nutrition and Health Connection

As most of you already know, we live in a cultural hypnosis that has somehow managed to convince us all that we're fragile, and it has taught us that drugs are the answer to all our problems.

We've been conditioned to feel awful about our bodies unless we're using the latest, greatest products on the market to stay healthy and fit.

The truth, however, is that we're anything BUT fragile. We don't need products and shakes and powders to keep us healthy and happy. Our natural state is one of energy, health, and strength.

Health and vitality comes from within, and it can also be lost from within.

When we take the simple act of eating, for example, it's easy to see how our self-love and self-esteem can be influenced by so many factors, and how it, in turn, can influence our external worlds.

Eating is something that we, as humans, HAVE to do every day, but the *way* we eat, the amounts of food we consume, that's a learned habit. Just like the thousand other little habits we do on a daily basis, food can either make us feel great, or it can break us.

Roughly 95% of what we do is an automatic response. It operates much like train track running through your brain. At the end of the day, that train track would have landed you at a destination, so if you want to start changing your life and working on your self-love, you have to change your beliefs, and as you know by now, we've discussed limiting beliefs in detail.

Just like the limiting beliefs you have about your self-esteem, you might also have a few limiting beliefs that keep you stuck on the same track as far as your nutrition goes, which might be keeping you overweight and feeling less-than-great about yourself.

Limiting Beliefs about Food that Break Down Self-Love

1. Thinking you have a great support system.
I'm not saying that your support system sucks, I'm merely suggesting you put some thought into whether or not your friends are really supportive of your health goals. If you're constantly surrounding yourself with people that indulge in unhealthy lifestyles, you're going to start subconsciously ignoring things that might be threatening your health goals.

2. Predicting the odds incorrectly.
Thinking that you're never going to feel better about yourself because you've just never been able to eat healthily is a major death-trap. There will always be a 50/50 opportunity. The odds never chance. The problem with humanity is that we're inclined to place too much value on what we've experienced in the past, believing that the past will always repeat itself, but you need to understand that the past does NOT equal the future.

- *You think you'll always have body issues because you can't find a way of committing to a healthy lifestyle*
- *Believing that large portions of food make you feel good*
- *Thinking that eating healthily will make you feel deprived*

- *Thinking that if you eat like all the 'skinny' girls, you'll fit in with them*
- *Believing that exercise is a punishment*
- *Believing that you're doomed because you come from an overweight family*
- *Thinking you don't have the willpower to make positive nutritional changes in your life*
- *Believing that there's something wrong with you*
- *Believing that you'll have loads of time to work on your body in the future*
- *Thinking that the way you feel, living in your body, doesn't affect your self-esteem*

If ever there was a time to change, it is now, and it all starts with changing your limiting beliefs.

You see, by not taking your relationship with food serious, you're opening yourself up to issues such as anxiety, depression, and even eating disorders, which don't help with self-love, at all.

Our world and westernized culture portray a sort of worship towards people with slim, toned bodies. Overweight people tend to be looked down on, and if you're unhappy about your body, it's easy to become depressed, because the culture makes it so obvious that not being in shape is totally undesirable.

We've already touched base on how the way we think can determine the quality of our lives, which means that it should go without saying that if we don't have healthy thoughts about food, there's no way it can empower us.

Because our thoughts affect our moods, they also play a role in determining our feelings and our behavior. When we can get to the core connection between our thoughts, emotions, moods, and our issues with food and how it makes us feel, it might unravel the way in which we can change our approach to our health goals.

Here are some of the subconscious mind patterns of overweight people:

- *Being overweight is a mind pattern of isolation. They think it protects them from the outside world and protects them from hurt.*
- *Being overweight can be a mind pattern of feeling empty inside.*
- *Being overweight can be an absence of self-love, a tell-tale sign of being unhappy with oneself.*
- *Being overweight can make them feel like they have a reason to procrastinate instead of going after what they want in life.*
- *Being overweight can be a mind pattern where they see eating as the only way they can assert their independence from their controlling parents who used to punish or reward them with food.*
- *They might see food as the only way they know to reward themselves.*
- *They might consider eating to be a quick way to change their state when they're feeling stressed or depressed.*

The Mindsets of Healthy People

When it comes to being healthy and having a great self-esteem thanks to their healthy habits, some people just tend to be gifted. The fact of the matter is that they have a whole different belief system, value system, and love themselves far more than unhealthy, overweight people do.

They have positive perspectives
We all have stress from time to time, but people that love themselves and their bodies realize every small opportunity for personal growth. They know how to handle stress and focus more on the things they can control in their lives.

They find pleasure in being healthy
Healthy people know that it didn't take them a day to set up a good relationship with food and their bodies, and they don't expect the impossible of themselves. They know that all things worth achieving in life take time. Instead of trying to find shortcuts on their journey towards wellbeing, they take in the entire experience wholeheartedly and accept their new lifestyles as a change for the better.

They eat to nourish their bodies as well as their minds
Food can either bring you pleasure, nourishment, healing, and social connections, or if you take the wrong approach, it can bring you heartache, obesity, eating disorders and hurt, and this is what healthy people know and keep in mind with their healthy lifestyles.

Why a healthy pH Balance is Essential for Loving Your Body

Our bodies are designed to get rid of acid, but our modern diets are crazy acidic, making it totally overwhelming for the body to get rid of all that acid.
Alkalizing and energizing are two key components of helping your body become healthy again so that you can start appreciating and loving it again, which can only lead to deeper self-love.

Our bodies operate on subtle electro-magnetic currents, and nerve signals that are electrical charges. With the help of pulses of electricity, the cells in our bodies are able to communicate with each other.

When we eat, our food is broken down into particles we call colloidals, and those particles are then carried to our cells on electrical charges. The food we consume can only provide value to our cells if they can be converted into the elements needed by your inner chemistry. The higher a food's electrical vibration, the higher our energy levels and the lower its electrical frequency, the less energy your body will get by eating that food.

Raw, unprocessed foods are high in energy. Fast foods and convenience meals, well you do the math.

To get back into the balance of things, you have to CLEANSE.

I'm NOT talking about a laxative here because those products all contain an abundance of acid, which you're trying to get rid of as well. I'm talking about super-hydrating the body with the help of water and 'green' drinks that have high energy levels.

I'll say it: Green smoothies look like swamp juice, and yes, they're an acquired taste, but for the amount of energy they provide, they're worth every single sip.

Most of us suffer from FLC Syndrome at one stage or another during our lives. It stands for Feel Like Crap Syndrome, and it comes with an abundance of nasty symptoms such as aching joints and muscles, a foggy brain, fatigue, headaches, allergies, and gas.

But here's the relatively easy solution and cure to the syndrome - DETOX.

Not detoxes where you have to take a bathroom break every 30 minutes or the one where you starve yourself for a week. The kind of detox I'm referring to here is a detox from sugar, and ultimately, everything that gets converted into sugar once inside the body.

Once you start eliminating all the sugar and sugary substances, you'll start sleeping better, have better moods, have improved digestion, and improved sexual desires and functions, and those are just the tip of the iceberg when it comes to the benefits of detox.

What are the benefits of detoxing?
1. *You'll feel more alive and full of energy after a detox*
2. *You'll lose excess weight*
3. *You'll banish bad cravings*
4. *You'll get a reboot because you're flushing out toxins such as sugar, caffeine, and alcohol*
5. *You'll have an opportunity of eliminating food sensitivities*
6. *You'll have better sex*
7. *You'll get back in touch with the roots of your motivation and choices for wanting to lead a healthier lifestyle*

Our bodies get rid of toxins in one of four ways:

Pee – We all know that the kidneys are responsible for flushing waste from the blood, so they need ENOUGH water to work at optimal levels. You should be drinking at least eight glasses of clean, fresh water a day.

Poop – One of the best ways to get rid of toxins in your body is to maintain at least one or two proper bowel movements a day. Bowel function really is something you DO have control over. To get things moving better, you can eat more fiber. Secondly, you can drink lots of water. You could also try taking some flax seed that has been grounded and even magnesium capsules to help things along.

Perspiration – Did you know that your skin is the single largest organ of elimination? In order to maximize your detox and sweat out all those chemicals, aim for at least 20 minutes of exercise three times a week (strenuous enough to make you build up a sweat though). You might also want to consider making use of a sauna, steam or detox bath to trigger your body's natural ability to detoxify itself through sweat.

Pranayama – This is the Indian word for Deep Breathing. The lungs are the unsung heroes of the body's detox squad, and with each breath you take, they bring in fresh oxygen and transport it throughout the body. Shallow breathing diminishes the power of the lungs by preventing oxygen from reaching all of your tissues. Deep breathing on the other hand deeply and fully oxygenates your brain, body, and spirit, totally transforming your health in the process. Belly breathing is simple. Start by putting your hand on your belly then breathe out, squeezing the air out of your lungs with your stomach muscles. Relax your stomach muscles as you breathe in after you have filled your lungs and try pushing your hand off your belly with your breath, filling the lower part of your lungs. Try doing this for 5 minutes a day

Self-Love and Illness / Disease

I lost my precious mother to cancer. She had two years of hell. She had a very rare cancer called "angiosarcoma" of the breast tissue. It started with a tiny little mark on her breast; I remember it looked like a ringworm.

She went to the doctor, and they said they didn't know what it was, but it should go away. It didn't!

It kept growing larger, and after three months, she went to her dermatologist who did a biopsy and confirmed she had "angiosarcoma."

My mother was so positive and sure she could beat this cancer. The same went for my family and me, we were also sure she could beat it. We didn't know anything about angiosarcoma at that stage, and we fought on.

If you're keen on learning more about the type of cancer my mother was diagnosed with, here's a crash course:
"Sarcoma" is not a word that is generally associated with discussions of breast cancer. A sarcoma is actually a cancerous tumor of connective or muscle tissues (myoepithelial cells), and generally, most breast tumors are "carcinoma" - which is a tumor of cancerous lining and membrane cells- (epithelial cells) such as the lining of the breast ducts.

An 'angio' sarcoma would indicate the involvement of blood supply elements in some way, and in fact, an angiosarcoma is basically a cancer of the cells which line the blood vessels. An angiosarcoma could, therefore, develop in virtually any area of the body, but a breast angiosarcoma usually starts in the cells which line the blood vessels of the breast or the underarm area.

The prognosis for breast angiosarcomas is variable, but it is a very serious diagnosis, especially if the tumor is of a high grade. It may be estimated that about 1/3 of women who develop breast angiosarcoma may not survive beyond three years following diagnosis, mostly due to metastasis of the disease to other areas of the body.

Barbara Marciniak states that love is what returns people to a state of health. It's something that captivated me, as I'm hoping it will do for you!

She says: "Understand that ill people are looking for love. There isn't enough love in their lives. It is LOVE that brings them back."

Dr. John Demartini confirms the healing power of love in his book ***The Breakthrough Experience:*** "I've worked with terminal cancer patients who had spontaneous remissions, and in each case, some form of love and gratitude came into their lives and shifted them. A spiritual experience transformed their illness. Even watching a movie about love has been shown to increase the levels of immunoglobulin A in the saliva, the body's first line of immunological defense. We get ill to teach us to love. It's not a punishment or a mistake. It's a gift. Illness is your body's way of telling you that you're lying about life. Every symptom and sign in your physical body is designed to reveal to you what you're lying about."

Psychological and Emotional Root Causes of Disease

Richard Moat describes the mindset that can lead to Cancer, as:

"You are likely to be a loving person who has repressed or withheld their (unacknowledged) feelings of bitterness and resentment; most often, these feelings are towards one particular parent; Most cancers are underpinned by unresolved, unexpressed anger. [...] You may be described as a 'rock' who handles and carries the problems of others (most often family), never complains and puts on a brave, unemotional face. If so, the version of you that you have been presenting to the world is unlikely to be the real you - it is more likely to be the you, you think you should be." (You can find out more at www.RichardMoat.com)

For further clues as to the source of Cancer, Richard advises you look up the part of the body in question. For example, his research indicates:

Breast cancer = Anger; Inter-family feuding; Low self-worth; Conflicted feelings.

Cervical cancer = Feeling inadequate and a failure; Angry at plans spoilt by others; Frustrated. No choice but to accept your lot; Feeling tied; Conflict of a sexual nature.

Colon cancer = Closed minded and rigid in thinking; Won't let go; Always battling something;

Kidney cancer = Feeling out of your depth, like an outcast, alone and abandoned;

Larynx cancer = A fear of being stifled or choked from living fully and freely.

Liver cancer = Fear of survival; Anger; Feeling as if 'territory' is under threat; Injustice, jealousy, and envy are likely under-currents

Lung cancer = Fear of dying, for self or someone else; Feeling threatened in a way that gives rise to fear and terror.

Pancreatic cancer = Resignation from abuse of trust and good nature; Feel the sweetness has gone out of life; A perceived threat to territory and concern of being unable to fulfill your expected role fully.

Prostate cancer = Intimate sexual conflict, often of an 'ugly' nature; Fear of loss of territory or valued person; threat to manhood, masculinity or role as husband/father.

Furthermore, Dr. Moat goes on to say that almost all health conditions are linked to emotional experiences. Here's a summary of what he points out as the root cause of most illnesses:

Acne = stems from low self-esteem, not accepting self, life seeming unfair, avoiding contact with others, buried feelings, guilt, difficulty facing up to something.

Addictions = stems from feeling emptiness, wanting to hide, avoiding problems, not trusting life's flow, lacking self-love; (addictions are an attempt to avoid or self-medicate our feelings).

Allergies = stems from intolerance and irritation of a particular person or behavior in others, internal conflict, over-sensitive, feeling easily intimidated, craving attention.

Alzheimer's Disease = stems from reality-avoidance tendencies, fear of the future, wishing to be cared for, thoughts of revenge, need to control others.

Anal problems = stems from repressed anger, unwillingness to let go, need for control, holding things back.

Arthritis = stems from having a critical nature, anger and bitterness, feeling unloved, low self-worth, fearing change, being inflexible and blame-oriented, stubborn, non-trusting.

Asthma = stems from having unclear boundaries, feeling inadequate, seeking control, excessive mother's love, feeling stifled, suppressing sadness, approval-seeking, fear of rejection, feeling unworthy.

Back problems = stems from feeling overloaded, carrying other's burdens, feeling held back, feeling unsupported, financial worries, concerns for one's survival.

Baldness = stems from feeling a sense of loss, protective of others, low self-worth, opinionated and controlling, frustration and worry.

Bladder Disorders = stems from bottling up feelings, feeling irritated and frustrated, fear of loss, holding on.

Bulimia = stems from guilt and low self-esteem, lacking unconditional love, rejecting yourself, challenging relationship with mother, desperate to control own feelings, longing to be free.

Cancer = stems from unexpressed anger, self-deprecation, deep hurt or long-standing resentment, lacking self-love, unforgiving. *(note: depending on the location of the Cancer, other issues could be at play. e.g. Kidney cancer = feeling like an outcast, alone and abandoned, fear for own survival).*

Diabetes = stems from a need for control, missing feeling loved or smothered with love, lack of ability to experience joy.

Eczema = stems from irritation and anger, a frustration continues unresolved, low in confidence, missing or longing for someone, boundaries not being respected.

Fibromyalgia = stems from chronic guilt, rigid and inflexible thinking and attitude, a 'victim' mentality, lacking confidence and creativity.

Headaches = stem from being self-critical, over-intellectualizing, restriction of self-expression, narrow-minded, fear of failure, controlling, not flowing with life, perfection-seeking, feeling under pressure to deliver, unexpressed strong feelings are surfacing, feeling continuously disappointed and let down.

Heart Attack = stem from materialistic tendencies, achievement-oriented, unforgiving, struggling to cope, emotionally detached, demanding high standards.

Infertility = can stem from unresolved early-years trauma, uncertainty around partner or parenting, fear of life change, underlying reluctance, responsibility aversion. *(Richard told me he has worked with 8 couples with infertility issues, and all of them got pregnant!)*

Kidney Stones = stems from holding on to long-standing thoughts, feelings, and attitudes that today serve no purpose, still living with past hurts; unshed tears that have calcified...

Liver Disorders = anger at injustices, powerlessness, judgmental and demanding of others, fault-finder, overly-corrosive emotional suppression.

Hyperthyroidism = always expending energy usually for others rather than yourself, feeling responsible (feeling obliged to engineer the lives of your loved ones), acting hastily, holding high expectations, fearing missing out.

Uterine Disorders = stems from feelings of fear or a guilt hangover, uncertainty, lack of self-acceptance, feeling pressured.

Pain = feeling deserving of punishment, guilt just under the surface, a longing to feel loved, self-critical, judgmental; an intelligent attempt by the body to avoid emotional pain.

How a Lack of Self-Love Might Impact Fertility

According to psychological studies, here might be a direct link between infertility and a lack of self-love and self-esteem.

Perhaps it is little surprise to hear people like spiritual chaneller Barbara Marciniak say that *"Loving yourself is the #1 thing you need to do to go forward in life."*

According to Stewart Swerdlow: *"Some people are afraid to have children because they do not want to recreate another version of themselves. They do not like themselves and fear another human being in the world who reflects that in their face all of the time."*

Of course anxiety, anger, suppression, and depression also have massive impacts on fertility, but it is interesting to note how the mindset of a woman, whether or not she dully accepts and deeply loves herself, can influence her fertility and ability to have children.

Findings revealed that infertile women group differed from fertile women group with respect to narcissism, dimensions of attachment style and uses of defence mechanism. The primary infertile group also showed marked difference from the secondary infertile group with respect to those variables.

A group of Indian researchers set out to evaluate the personality features of people who were infertile and found that there was a marked difference between fertile and infertile people.

"Women with functional infertility (i.e. not organic) had low scores on cooperativeness and self-directedness than women with organic infertility.

A sense of personal failure, guilt and shock are also found to be important factors that hinder the process of a successful pregnancy.

It has also been found that women suffering from infertility of unknown biological cause tend to have an avoidant attachment style. The infertile group have high discomfort with closeness and are more preoccupied with relationships whereas the fertile group is far more confident about their relationships as compared to the infertile women.

So how do infertile women measure up to fertile women?
From all the research that was conducted, infertile women had an 11% higher depression rate than fertile women.

They also showed roughly 12% higher levels of anxiety, which significantly impacts their overall psychological wellness.

How can you reclaim a healthy body with love?
It might sound simple, but simple techniques often have the greatest of impacts in our lives. Here are my top tips for reclaiming your healthy body with love:

- *Make friends with the person in the mirror. Look at yourself in the mirror and say, "You are perfect and beautiful just the way you are."*

- *Do a Body Blessing prayer every day.*

    The body blessing prayer starts with a modified Yoga Hero Pose, because you are a hero. Your body is the physical manifestation of the hero in you. Your body is the path to oneness of body, mind and soul. Your body is a window to your Soul. Health and healing cannot come until you love your body:

1.Starting in the Hero Pose, open your hands with your palms upward, representing your openness to receive Love and blessings from above.
2.Bow your head.
3.As you breathe in deeply, slowly bring your open palms up toward your shoulders.
4.As you move your arms upward, scooping up Divine Love, you will bring your open palms towards yourself, touching yourself lightly on the shoulder to symbolize your receiving and excepting Love from the Universal Source.
5.Slowly lower your arms again as you exhale and bow your head.
6.Repeat as often as needed to feel the blessing and to love your body!

https://youtu.be/r0-o8RLhQRA

- *Honour the perfect spirit within you with beautiful foods.*
- *Make food an offering to your amazing self.*
- *Add green juice to your diet.*
- *Only eat when you're hungry. Listen to your body. Eat slowly. When you no longer feel truly hungry, stop eating.*
- *Be mindful of what you put in your mouth. Remember, your body is your temple.*
- *Avoid emotional eating. If you feel something you don't wish to feel, be brave enough to be with that feeling.*
- *Move your beautiful body. Even if you can only manage a slow 20-minute walk per day, do it.*
- *Use affirmations*
- *Use visualizations*

Believe in yourself. Love yourself. Be whole. You know you already are.

Exercise

It's time to grab that journal again. Now that you have a better understanding of the limiting beliefs that could be getting between you, health, and ultimately, self-love, it's time to identify them.

Answer the following questions:

1. Why would a part of me believe that I need this illness/injury/situation/challenge in my life?

2. If I give this up and decide to get healthy, who won't be punished anymore that I think should be?

3. Who would it hurt if I got over this issue?

4. Do I feel more powerful in some ways with this problem?

5. Does letting go of this mean that I am forgetting something, or forgiving someone?

6. What would I lose without this "story" to my life? What is the downside?

7. What do I think I have to do to make this situation go away? Is there a downside to that?

During my own healing process, I'd often ask myself: "If my brain had some crazy idea of why I shouldn't heal, what would it be?" You'd be surprised what answers might come to you!

This exercise should have left you with a range of possible limiting beliefs that could be getting in the way of your true happiness. The subconscious mind usually has a lot of "great" (that's what it thinks) ideas on why we shouldn't overcome our challenges, so isn't it time you started challenging your mind?

CHAPTER 6

How Your Relationships are Affected by Your Self-Love

Here's a touching, less-than-charming love story that paved my way to success in relationships…

The moon was shining brightly that balmy summer's night in the park. He'd arranged a meeting to "sort things out." Little did he know I'd finally built the courage to walk away. And that's exactly what I did.

I was devastated but mostly relieved. Finally, I was free.

For the longest time, I'd craved his love. I needed his approval. I wanted the happy ending so badly.

Why? I meant something when I was with him. I felt worthy and kind of secure.

But I wasn't. I'd given away all of my power. I was dependent on him to feel love.

And he knew it, so he treated me however he wanted. For him, it was a game, and every problem in our relationship somehow always came back to me.

I was needy, insecure, and completely out of touch with who I was and what I really wanted. I'd sacrificed everything about me in an effort to try to please another being.

He told me I wasn't sexy enough, so I read book after book about how to be more feminine and alluring.

He told me I was too quiet, so I went out of my way to be outgoing, happy, and bubbly.

He told me I took up too much time, so I made other plans and disappeared for a while.

He could have told me anything, and I would have accepted it.

There wasn't an ounce of self-respect in my bones. My misery was born from this very fact.

I'd let this happen for so long. It wasn't entirely his fault. My neediness and lack of self-worth had created and perpetuated our problems. But for some reason that I can't explain, that evening, a spark had been ignited, and I'd finally had enough.

I'd reached my pain threshold.

I was completely done with feeling miserable, doubting myself, and feeling disrespected.

I was so over letting someone else control my decisions, emotions, and self-worth.

I'd begun to love myself a little more than I loved him. A butterfly was emerging from the cold, dark cocoon I'd been hiding in my whole life. It felt new and scary but ridiculously empowering and liberating.

In a moment of clarity a string of epiphanies melted my confusion:
- *Deep love comes from within.*
- *I choose how I want to feel.*
- *I'll never be satisfied just with love from someone else.*
- *If I don't authentically love myself, I can't expect anyone else to love me truly.*
- *The way I treat myself shows others how I expect to be treated.*

That evening I vowed to put myself first and to be kind, loving, and generous with myself. This is the way I wanted to be treated. Out of self-respect and needing a fresh start, I walked away. From that point on it was my intention to live my life on my terms.

It might sound selfish, but it was completely the opposite.

The Real Impact of Neediness on Relationships

I wholeheartedly believe that sharing the joys and wonder of life with another being who lights up your world is absolutely priceless. There's nothing like it. It's one of the greatest joys on Earth, and something every human being deserves to experience.

But it's extremely hard to find this happiness with another if you're in a relationship just for the sake of having one or more of your needs filled up by somebody else.

Being needy, insecure, and trying to gain approval and a sense of self-worth from your partner puts a huge amount of pressure on them, and it's a major turn-off.

The truth is that you'll never be able to gain self-worth by looking to find it from someone else. It's an unachievable task because feeling inherently loved and worthy comes from within. Not from your partner.

An outstanding love doesn't come from two half-fulfilled people coming together to make one whole, complete life. Outstanding love comes from two whole people coming together to share and enhance their already full and beautiful lives.

An amazing relationship comes about when we own and appreciate who we are and completely accept the other person for who they are.

So loving and putting yourself first is not selfish, it's necessary. It's imperative to creating the wonderful love and life we all desire.

And let's get something straight - loving yourself doesn't deplete the love tank; it actually fills it up, so we have even more to give.

What Happens to Relationships When You Don't Love Yourself

1. You create extra work for your partner.
If you don't love yourself, you'll be making the work twice as hard on your partner because essentially, they'll have to pick up that slack and carry your weight. Your partner will have to work extra hard to make you happy when you're struggling with self-doubt and low self-esteem. And sometimes, despite their best efforts to give you the love and support you need, it still won't be good enough for you.

2. You accept bad treatment.
Some people allow their partners to just walk all over them, and it happens because they enter relationships without first loving themselves. Because they have low self-esteem, they're more likely to accept abusive, neglectful, and inappropriate treatment because they don't think they deserve anything better.

People who lack self-love live in fear that they'll be abandoned and lack intrinsic self-confidence, which leads to the acceptance of poor treatment. When we don't have a strong internal sense of self-confidence, it leads to the feeling of "*I'm not worthy*" or a feeling that we don't deserve our partner.

People that lack in self-love also tend to rate their partners higher than they rate themselves, which is why they accept the fact that their partners constantly criticize them, act selfishly, and don't give them the love and effort they truly deserve.

The only way to escape this trap is to start treating yourself like your own best friend again, as someone you genuinely want to be around, someone you want to protect, and someone you want to serve. If your partner doesn't treat you like you deserve to be treated, it's not a relationship you need in your life.

3. You'll start imagining the worst possible scenarios.
It's easy to imagine that things in the relationship are going awful if you don't have high self-esteem or you lack self-love. You might also mistakenly think that intentions and circumstances are worse than they

actually are. This might be a tell-tale sign of self-projected insecurities, which does not happen if you truly love yourself. By believing in negative outcomes, you're attracting negative outcomes.

4. You'll compare your relationship to others.
Self-doubt will see you comparing the way your partner treats you to the way your friends' partner treats them. Your decision to compare and resent your partner's behavior is just a means for you to project your insecurities. If you love yourself enough, you'll be living a life that shows your partner how you want to be treated, instead of waiting around and expecting them to live up to standards you never really put out there, to begin with.

5. Your stickiness will wear off.
The importance of self-love in a relationship can be compared to a sticker. Imagine you're a brand new sticker, and you've never been used. You're untouched undamaged, unattached, and in perfect condition. You're super sticky. You could basically stick to anything, and you'd instantly form a super strong bond and stay put without any issues.

But then you get rejected, undervalued, caught up in self-hate, blinded by limiting beliefs, and every time that happens, you lose some of your stickiness. Every time you engage in negative thoughts, self-hate, self-sabotage, or dysfunctional relationships, you get less sticky.

Each time you attempt to stick onto someone new, it gets easier and easier to pull away because connections become harder and harder to form. This is true for platonic and romantic relationships.

And like a sticker that's been pulled off the surface and has been used, the connections you form won't be nearly as strong as they once were. But if there were ever a way to somehow get sticky again, it would be through self-improvement and self-betterment.

You can only ever bring positivity into a relationship (and attract great relationships) if you truly love yourself.

What Does Self-Love Really Look Like?

It's prioritizing your dreams and making an effort to do things that inspire and light you up.

It's saying no to things you don't agree with or that don't fit in with your plans.

It's deciding to spend time with people who support, encourage, and motivate you to be the best version of you.

It's owning your thoughts and opinions and refusing to be swayed in order to please others.

It's being gentle with and talking kindly and sweetly to yourself.

It's having the courage to try new things that you've always wanted to experience.

It's taking time out to nourish your mind, body, and soul—exercise, eating well, alone time.

It's trusting your intuition and honoring your own truth.

Its spending money on things that make you feel amazing while investing in your future.

It's daring to believe that you're capable of achieving and creating the life you visualize.

It's choosing to see the good and refusing to let others bring you down.

It's gifting yourself forgiveness and accepting yourself for all of your beautiful and not-so-cool quirks and qualities.

How Does Self-Love Create A Great Relationship?

When we truly love and respect ourselves, we're free from doubt and endless worry, so we trust our feelings and decisions. It allows us to be courageous and authentic.

We begin to live from the heart and play a bigger, kinder, more generous version of life. We forget our self-imposed boundaries and dare to dream larger and wilder.

We stop focusing on negativity and become present to the beauty and possibilities within and outside of ourselves. We realize how great our lives are and open the doors for gratitude to flow in abundance.

We start to emanate happiness, confidence, playfulness, peace, and positivity. It's electric and like a powerful magnet to others. Your ideal partner will be drawn to you like a bear fresh out of hibernation looking for his first meal.

And once you find that special one, love will be easy. It'll be natural. It'll flow freely without judgment or pretense. It'll inspire and nourish you. Your lives will be even richer, happier, and more vibrant than ever.

And you'll wonder why you didn't take the time to fall radically in love with you just a little bit sooner.

How do you see yourself? This is an important question, because how you see yourself is how you see everything. If you don't love yourself, you can't genuinely love someone else. If you can't accept yourself, you won't be able to accept others.

If you don't have compassion for yourself, then you'll have no compassion for others.

If you can't forgive yourself, you won't be able to sincerely forgive others.

That's why increasing self-love is crucial for healthy relationships! A healthy sense of self-love will improve your relationship with yourself, which will improve your relationships with others.

There's nothing that can interfere with an authentic, reciprocal relationship quite like low self-esteem can. If you don't believe you are good enough, how can you ever believe that a loving partner could choose you?

When you don't love yourself, you'll be testing or sabotaging relationships that have real potential, or on the flip side, you could end up staying in a relationship that doesn't serve you, that doesn't see you being treated in a way that matches your beliefs about yourself.

The relationship that you have with yourself sets the bar for every other relationship you'll have in your life. If you've been struggling to maintain happy and healthy relationships, it might be because you aren't happy with yourself.

When we enter relationships while our minds are clouded with insecurities and feelings of inadequacy, our romantic relationships are doomed to be dysfunctional. Our insecurities are more influential on our partners than we might think. Not only will you be exhausting your partner with your constant need for validation, attention, and reassurance, but it further destroys your self-esteem.

The art of loving oneself is a learned and practiced way of life. Without mastering self-love first, your romantic relationships will suffer a noticeable disconnect.

> *"We lose ourselves in the things we love. We find ourselves, there too." -Kristin Martz*

CHAPTER 7

How Advertising Exploits Your Emotional Vulnerabilities

How Marketing Makes You Unhappy

It's a little-known fact: Advertising unashamedly fosters unhappiness with oneself and with one's possessions. In fact, the very purpose of advertising is to make people feel that without this or that product, they are inferior. Without the latest and greatest, they are less than or not good enough, not cool enough, and that they are defective.

It's crazy how we've become conditioned to want to keep up with the Jones'.

In the words of a contemporary advertising executive: "Advertising, at its best, is about making people feel that without their product, you're a loser…You open up the emotional vulnerabilities in consumers through advertising, and that's how you convince them to buy your product."

If you're constantly made to feel "not good enough", you're going to want to buy more stuff so that you have stuff that jazzes up your other stuff, which can make you look cooler than the guy next door.

This is particularly glaring in women's magazines. In Jean Kilbourne's excellent book - Can't Buy My Love - she makes the following observation about advertising:

- Advertising is one of the most powerful forces in our society. Advertising is part of the environment you live in, and this environment has been polluted.

- Advertising shapes our values, our attitudes, our culture, and defines our dreams, even if we don't think it works on us. We are all influenced by advertising. There is no way to tune out this much information, especially when it is designed to break through the 'tuning out' process.

- The bankrupt values of advertising —organized around money and driven by hype— corrupt our true values, relationships, and commitment to civic life.

- Ads create an environment in which bad choices are constantly reinforced (addiction, fast food, smoking and drinking, narcissism and selfishness, etc.).

- Ads reinforce that human relationships are fragile, difficult, and disappointing but products won't let us down. ("Who says guys are afraid of commitment? He's had the same backpack for years."; "The ski instructor faded away three years ago, but the sweater didn't."; to children: "This toy doll is your new best friend!")

- The main message of advertising is that happiness comes from products, not relationships.

- Advertising corrupts relationships and then offers us products as solace and as substitutes for human connection we long for.

- Ads encourage us to objectify each other and to believe that our most significant relationships are with products. Ads leave us romantic about objects and deeply cynical about humans.

- Advertising contributes greatly to a climate in which relationships flounder and addictions flourish. Relationships are constantly devalued. Kilbourne writes: "I believe there is a connection between the throwaway world of advertising and today's throwaway approach to marriage. All too often our market-driven culture locks people into adolescent fantasies of sex and relationships. And there is a connection between the constant images of instant sexual gratification and passion and the increasing burden on marriage and long-term lovers."

- Advertisers use psychological research to target children (because if you hook them early, they are yours for life).

- "I am raising my daughter in a culture that is entirely materialistic, that co-opts spiritual values and movements for social change and uses them to sell her jeans and cigarettes. I am raising her in a culture that trivializes relationships and encourages her to envy her friends and compete with them."

- "Our materialistic culture encourages [suffering from a sense of emptiness] because people who feel empty make great consumers. The emptier we feel, the more likely we are to turn to products, to fill us up, to make us feel whole ... They all serve to distance us from our feelings and to deflect attention from that which might really make a difference in our lives."

- Ads steer us away from what really makes us happy: "meaningful work, authentic relationships, and a sense of connection with history, community, nature, and the cosmos."

Creating A Model That Is Virtually Impossible To Attain

"Infotainment is used for programming and conditioning the public. This medium is far more effective for subliminal reinforcement of desired attitudes towards our objectives. We reinforce the desired norm through advertising, creating a model for

people to live up to, that is virtually impossible to attain. The result is an incomplete, desperate individual seeking acceptance."

American media insider

Depression Is a Rational Response to a Sick Society

I believe that the values of materialism promoted by mass media today (to the detriment of spiritual values), and the resultant loss of belief in God, are to blame for the surge in instances of depression. The Advertising industry and mass media have subverted and corrupted our traditional values. They have perverted and corrupted every aspect of our daily life, for the sake of promoting 'consumerism'.

British psychologist Oliver James's research, points to the fact that the era of 'Selfish Capitalism' unleashed by mass media advertising in the 1930s caused an epidemic of the 'Affluenza' virus. This is what he calls the set of values we see today in Western people, such as placing a high value on acquiring money and possessions, looking good in the eyes of others, and wanting to be famous (essentially, materialistic values which lead to egregious consumption). It is useful to remember that these values are not innate to human beings. They've been programmed into us. Oliver writes:

> "Infection with the Affluenza Virus increases your susceptibility to the commonest emotional distresses: depression, anxiety, substance abuse and personality disorders (e.g. 'me, me, me' narcissism, febrile moods, or confused identity). We have become absolutely obsessed with measuring ourselves and others through the distorted lens of Affluenza values. The great majority of people in English-speaking nations now define their lives through earnings, possessions, appearance and celebrity, and those things are making them miserable because they impede the meeting of our fundamental needs."

In other words, the more materialistic a society becomes, the more its inhabitants become depressed, anxious, and they don't know who they even are anymore.

A 2004 study by the World Health Organization highlighted the shocking fact that over 26% of Americans had suffered from some form of emotional distress in the previous 12 months (such as depression, anxiety, substance abuse), SIX times more than Nigerians, who were forty times poorer than America. America, he notes, is by some margin the most emotionally distressed of all nations.

Oliver James presents two interesting conclusions. The first is that depression and anxiety are normal in a society bombarded by unfettered advertising and consumeristic values:

> "It is grossly inaccurate to depict depression, anxiety, and other psychoses as diseases requiring medical treatment. [...] most emotional distress is best understood as a rational response to sick societies. Change those societies, and we will all be less distressed."

In other words, change the environment, and depression and anxiety will become rarer occurrences. There are 350 million people suffering from depression around the world, according to the World Health Organization, and this is not caused by some 'chemical imbalance' in their brains. This is caused by the fact that our society is profoundly sick and corrupted.

His second conclusion is even more poignant: religion or spiritual beliefs can immunize people against the effects of this materialistic 'virus'. Indeed, people who believe in something beyond our physical world are far less likely to suffer from depression and unhappiness.

> "Wherever I went I found that religion seemed to be a powerful vaccine. Much to the consternation of social scientists, on average, regular churchgoers suffer less depression or unhappiness than non-believers. Almost

> by definition, religious people are less likely to be materialistic and to have fewer goals or motivations and more likely to be preoccupied with things spiritual. One study of 860 young American adults, showed this very clearly. Those with materialistic values, such as wanting money or prestige, were far less likely to be religious, and they were unhappier, drank and smoked more, and, in the case of the women, were at greater risk of eating disorders."

No surprise there, since people afflicted by a 'Philosophy of Futility' and materialistic values tend to use consumption to fill the spiritual void they are feeling. But you cannot consume your way to happiness.
Source: God, The Meaning of Life, And What Happens After You Die – Mark Anastasi

"Any thought that you continue to think is called a belief. And many of your beliefs serve you extremely well…but some of your beliefs do not serve you well: Thoughts about your own inadequacy or your unworthiness are examples of those kinds of thoughts…Here is a process that can give you the immediate benefit of changing your beliefs in a much shorter time. We call this the process of Meditation.

We teach the process of Meditation because it is easier for most of you to clear your minds, having no thought, than it is for you to think pure, positive thoughts. For when you quiet your mind, you offer no thought; and when you do so, you offer no resistance; and when you have activated no resistant thought, the vibration of your Being is high and fast and pure"
Ask & It Is Given, Esther & Jerry Hicks

They're Controlling the Masses!
In his documentary - The Century of Self - Adam Curtis highlighted how Sigmund Freud had discovered, at the turn of the 20th century, that humans had primitive, sexual, ad aggressive forces hidden deep inside their subconscious minds, and that if those forces were not controlled, it could lead to the chaos and destruction of societies.

At that time, the ruling class saw this as proof that humans could not be trusted with rational decision making, which meant that democracy was not a good idea. "They" rationalized and decided that humans needed an iron fist to rule them.

In the 1920s Freud's nephew Edward Bernays brought his uncle's ideas to America, and put them to use for the benefit of US corporations. He had been impressed at how successfully propaganda had been used to entice American men to enlist and fight in Europe in the First World War. While the British abandoned propaganda in peace time, the Americans continued and expanded its use with the help of Bernays, who argued that American public opinion must be engineered from above to 'control the rabble'. He considered the average person to be *stupid, incapable of rational thinking.*
He couldn't use the term 'propaganda', as it had a negative connotation. Since the war, people had realised that propaganda had been used to deceive the public into acquiescing to the government's agenda. It was basically misleading, dishonest and exploitative. So Bernays called it 'Public Relations', creating a new industry in the process.

The political writer Walter Lippmann argued that "if human beings were driven by unconscious, irrational forces, then it was necessary to re-think democracy." The government needed to manage 'the bewildered herd' through psychological techniques that would control the unconscious feelings of the masses. Bernays put forward the following theory: "<u>by stimulating people's inner desires and then sating them with consumer products you can manage the irrational force of the masses.</u>"

They would sublimate their inner, primitive, sexual and aggressive forces through the consumption of goods. He called it *"The engineering of consent"*. Its aims would be achieved through clever, subtle, and pervasive propaganda aimed at controlling the minds of the unknowing public.

One of Bernays' first successes was in reengineering how women felt about smoking. George Washington Hill, president of the American

Tobacco Company, hired Edward Bernays in 1928 to lead a campaign to entice more women to smoke in public. At that time there was a taboo against women smoking, because, in the minds of people, it was associated with prostitution. Psychoanalyst Abraham Brille told Bernays: "Cigarettes are a symbol of the penis and of male sexual power. If you can find a way to connect cigarettes with the idea of challenging male power, then women will smoke because then they would have their own penises."

Bernays decided to stage an event at the 1928 New York Easter day parade. He persuaded a group of rich, fashionable upper-class young women to hide cigarettes under their clothes, and light them up dramatically on his prompt. He had informed the press that suffragettes were protesting for the right to vote, by lighting up 'torches of freedom'... The pictures were all over the press across America the next day. Bernays managed to make women associate smoking with the idea that it made them more powerful and independent, a ridiculous idea that persists to this day.

Bernays also persuaded female film stars to smoke ostentatiously on screen, thus endorsing cigarettes as respectable and desirable. Thanks to his psychological mass mind control methods, he had successfully associated *smoking* with feelings of independence, power, glamour, and freedom. Women throughout the world began to smoke in their millions. **The idea that smoking actually *made* women freer, was complete nonsense, of course. It was irrational.** Women were just being exploited and made poorer and unhealthy by becoming addicts to cigarettes, enriching Big Tobacco in the process. Tobacco use has killed over 100 million people in the 20th century, more than all deaths in World Wars I and II combined.

This experiment made Bernays realize that **it is possible to persuade people to behave irrationally – *even do something that kills you* – if you link a product to people's subconscious desires and feelings.** He had proven to American corporations that they could make people want things they didn't need, through psychological manipulation. This got them *very* interested indeed…

In the 1930s leading Wall Street banker Paul Mazer wrote: "We must shift America from a 'needs' to a 'desires' culture. People must be trained to desire, to want new things even before the old had been entirely consumed. We must shape a new mentality in America. Man's desires must overshadow his needs."

The New York banks funded the creation of chains of department stores across America, which would display the new consumer products, while **Bernays was tasked by the banks with creating a 'consumer culture',** through the promotion of fashion in women's magazines, press releases about new products, product placement in movies, celebrity endorsements, and many more of the mass consumer persuasion techniques that we see today.

They also tasked Bernays with **remaking the image of 'Big Business'**, seen up until then as the exploiters of the working class. Under the aegis of The National Association of Manufacturers, an organization consisting of all the major corporations in the US, a major PR campaign was launched on a grand scale (it is ongoing to this day), using every channel possible, and every technique possible, to program the population with the following concepts: corporations are inevitable and indispensable; corporations create jobs; corporations are much more efficient than governments; corporations are responsible for progress; corporations create the products that make your life better; corporate successes and domination are to be celebrated. Unfortunately, none of these statements are true.
Source - Mark Anastasi

Advertising is Hijacking Your Brain and Making You Unhappy
Since the dawn of capitalist ventures, successful marketing has always been targeting human psychology and using it to its benefit. Before we understood what their actual goals were, we probably all believed that marketers understood and cared about our needs.

In Vance Packard's book - Hidden Persuaders - which was released in 1957, the author uncovered how influential psychology and behavioral science was becoming to advertising agencies. Advertisers have always been trying to pinpoint the impulsive and sometimes destructive causes for purchases that consumers make.

Since the 1950's, the game hasn't changed, in fact, it only got worse. With more data, algorithm sophistication, and hyper-optimizations of ads, it's now easier than ever for advertising to manipulate your instincts.

How Advertising Creates Perceived Needs
Abraham Maslow's Hierarchy of Needs, which dates back to 1943, breaks down the road to a person's self-actualization. The first step is where physiological needs such as food, water, and shelter, are met. Then there are safety needs - which is security - followed by love needs, where we all have a need to feel like we're loved and that we belong. Fourth on the ladder is esteem needs, where we get a sense of accomplishment and prestige, and it is only when all of those needs are met, that individuals feel like they've reached their full potential.

You see advertising targets the most basic of psychological demands, playing off denial of our access to those needs. A simple example would be food. The desire for food will always be there, but marketers manipulate the psyche to get us to believe that the requirement is unmet if we don't purchase a *specific* product, whether it's the cheeseburger they're trying to sell or a new candy bar.

How Advertising Hijacks Fear Aversion
According to Martin Lindstrom, author of the book Buyology, human fear overrides any other purchasing behavior. Marketers use fear, uncertainty, and doubt to stoke a sense of fear in consumers by creating urgency for their products.

The ads that are most successful are the ones that get consumers to take a quick call to action. When people feel a sense of urgency, they don't process or scrutinize information correctly.

How Advertising Makes Us All Unhappy
All this psychological dilly-dallying and coercion isn't the worst effect that marketing has on consumers. According to research, when it

comes to choice and happiness, our levels of choice (or perceived choice) might be increasing, but so are our levels of unhappiness.

According to Barry Schwartz, all of this choice has two effects, two negative effects on people. One effect, paradoxically, is that it produces paralysis, rather than liberation. The second effect is that even if we manage to overcome the paralysis and make a choice, we end up less satisfied with the result of the choice than we would be if we had fewer options to choose from.

Prolonged exposure to so much choice is not liberating us from suffering, but likely making it worse. The nature of consumption, advertising, and human psychology means that as soon as we make a decision, we are reminded of what we did NOT choose or that we could have chosen BETTER.

We immediately feel the compounded opportunity costs of our decisiveness and begin regretting our choice and the regret is particularly effective when contextual advertising reminds us of what we did not choose.

But does advertising guide us to resolve these negative feelings? Of course if does, with promises that more consumption will ensure us that we're not missing out on 'the good life.'

How Facebook was Designed to Exploit Human Vulnerability

Facebook's founding president, Sean Parker, became a billionaire thanks to the social media craze, but he turns around and says "God only knows what it's doing to our children's brains."

He also stated that the social media platform probably interferes with productivity in weird ways.

When the creators of Facebook first started the platform, they knew very well how they were exploiting a vulnerability in human psychology. Not only did Facebook change our relationship with society and with each other, but it also affected the relationship that people had with themselves.

Facebook, and any social media platform for that matter is a social-validation feedback loop, and if our minds can be hijacked, our choices really aren't as free as we think they are!

Why the Media Makes It Hard to Love Yourself

If you had to sit 20 millennials down in a room and ask them to honestly say how many of them love themselves, I can almost guarantee that around half of them will raise their hands. But the other half?

For them, it's just too hard to love themselves when they don't feel like they're special, like there's a specific reason why they need to love themselves. And here's why:

1. We are conditioned to belief that self-care equals self-love

Self-love is not something you'll gain by going for a massage or getting your hair done. We call those self-care activities, and they'll only make you feel worse if you don't already love yourself because if you spend money on something you do not love, you're creating a pitfall for guilt.

2. Someone told us that self-love equals being selfish or egotistical

There is unfortunately a fine - and I mean very fine - line between being egotistical and loving yourself. You just need to understand that line and get to a place and space where you're able to wholeheartedly accept who you are and love everything you are and are capable of.

With the age of social media, this becomes an even more prominent problem. The web is flooded with images of perfect girls with toned bodies, flawless skin, and faces that will never need makeup in their life. And the guys? They're masculine, ripped, and look like they walked straight out of a Men's Health cover shoot.

Then you start comparing yourself to them. Your face has old acne scars. Your hair looks like a lion's mane on a good day. Your wardrobe is six seasons old, and your luck with the opposite sex just doesn't seem to exist.

But here's the deal: If you love yourself, unconditionally, you don't have to care about the world out there. You only need your own approval. I say it's time to take a step away from the computer, or your smartphone, and just start focusing on yourself again. There's nobody in the world that can compare to you, so just accept yourself and love yourself for who you truly are!

The Seven Steps to Finally Loving Yourself

CHAPTER 8

Tools

Test to Help You Find Out Who You Are and Why You Should Love Yourself

I used a few tests to help me discover my values as well as my specific personality type. I reckon that the Demartini Value Determination Process and the Myers-Briggs Personality Type Indicator are valuable tools that might be able to help you find out more about who you are and what makes you tick. Go ahead and do these tests. I've also included the Fear of Success Scale, which should help you determine how fearful you are of achieving success in life. I promise you'll have a better self-understanding of your personality once you've completed them, and they'll also give you so many more reasons to love yourself!

The Demartini Value Determination Process®

Determine your values, step by step

The Demartini Value Determination Process® developed by Dr. John Demartini, author, educator, leadership and performance specialist.

This is a multi-step process in which you keep refining your answers until your hierarchy of values finally emerges with crystal clarity.

Step One:
Answer the following 13 questions

1. How do you fill your personal space?
Have you ever noticed how things that are really not important to you go into the trash, the attic, or the storage closet? By contrast, you keep the things that are important to you where you can see them, either at home or at work.
What does your life demonstrate through your space?
When you look around your home or office, do you see family photos, sports trophies, business awards, books?
Do you see beautiful objects, comfortable furniture for friends to sit on, or souvenirs of favorite places you've visited?
Perhaps your space is full of games, puzzles, DVDs, CDs, or other forms of entertainment.
Whatever you see around you is a very strong clue as to what you value most.

What 3 things fill your space?
_____
_____
_____
_____

2. How do you spend your time?
Here's something you can count on: people always make time for things that are really important to them and run out of time for things that aren't.
Even though people usually say, "I don't have time for what I really want to do," the truth is that they are too busy doing what is truly most important to them.

And what they think they want to be doing isn't really what's most important. You always find time for things that are really important to you. Somehow, you figure it out.

So how do you spend your time?

I personally spend my days researching, writing, networking and having positive thoughts. Those are my four highest values.

I always find time for doing them.

And I almost never find time for cooking, doing domestic things and watching television which are low on my list of values.

How you spend your time tells you what matters to you most.

In which three ways do you spend your time?
_____
_____
_____
_____

3. How do you spend your energy?

You always have energy for things that inspire you – the things you value most. You run out of energy for things that don't.

Things that are low among your values drain you; things that are high among your values energize you.

In fact, when you are doing something that you value highly, you have more energy at the end of the day than when you started because you're doing something that you love and are inspired by.

So how do you spend your energy – and where do you get your energy?

In which three ways do you spend your energy and where do you feel energized?
_____
_____
_____
_____

4. How do you spend your money?

Again, you always find money for things that are valuable to you, but you never want to part with your money for things that are not important to you. So your choices about spending money tell you a great deal about what you value most.

Now, at this point, you might be noticing some overlap: some similarities between what you fill your space with and how you spend your time, energy, and money.

That is healthy. It means that you have already aligned a lot of your values, goals, and daily activities.

If you notice a lot of divergence between the answers to these first four questions, you might benefit from bringing your values and goals into deeper alignment.

In which three ways do you spend your money?

_____
_____
_____
_____

5. Where do you have the most order and organization?

We tend to bring order and organization to things that are important to us and to allow chaos with things that are low on our values.

So look at where you have the greatest order and organization in your life, and you'll have a good sense of what matters most to you.

In my case, I see the most order and organization in my research and writing, and in my networking with people.

This helps me see that my values involve research, writing, people and mind work.

In which three areas are you most organized?

_____
_____
_____
_____

Chapter 8: Tools

6. Where are you most reliable, disciplined, and focused?

You never have to be reminded from the outside to do the things that you value the most.

You are inspired from within to do those things and so you do them. Look at the activities, relationships, and goals for which you are disciplined, reliable, and focused – the things that nobody has to get you up to do.

For me, again, that's researching, writing, networking, speaking, meditating and doing mind work. I love those things!

In which three activities and areas are you most reliable disciplined and focused?

_____
_____
_____
_____
_____

7. What do you think about, and what is your most dominant thought?

I'm not talking about the negative self-thought or the things that distract you. I'm not talking about the fantasies, "shoulds," or "ought's."

I'm talking about your most common thoughts about how you want your life to be – thoughts that you show slow or steady evidence of actually bringing to fruition.

What are your three most dominant thoughts?

_____
_____
_____
_____
_____

8. What do you visualize and realize?

Again, I'm not talking about fantasies.

I'm asking what you visualize for your life that is slowly but surely coming true. In my case, I visualize travelling the world and setting foot in every country on the face of the Earth.

That is what I visualize. And that is what I am realizing.

So what are you visualizing and realizing?

What are the three ways you visualize your life?

_____
_____
_____
_____

9. What is your internal dialogue?

What do you keep talking to yourself about the most? I am not asking about negative self-talk or self-aggrandizement.

I want you to think of your preoccupation with what you desire most – intentions that actually seem to be coming true and showing some fruits.

What are the three things that you have internal dialogues about?

_____
_____
_____
_____

10. What do you talk about in social settings?

Okay, now here's a clue that you'll probably notice for other people as well as yourself.

What are the topics that you keep wanting to bring into the conversation that nobody has to remind you to talk about?

What subjects turn you into an instant extrovert?

Whether your 'baseline' personality is extrovert or introvert, you've probably noticed that there are topics that immediately bring you to

life and start you talking and others that turn you into an introvert who has nothing to say – or make you want to change the subject.
You can use this same insight to analyze other people's values.
If you go up to somebody and they ask you about your kids that means their kids are important to them.
If they say, "How's business?" they value business.
If they ask, "Are you seeing anyone new?", then relationships matter to them.
Topics that attract you are a key to what you value.

What are the three things that you speak about in social settings?
_____
_____
_____
_____

_____

11. What inspires you?

What inspires you now? What has inspired you in the past? What is common to the people who inspire you? Figuring out what inspires you most reveals what you value most.

What are the three things that inspire you the most?
_____
_____
_____
_____

_____

12. What are the most consistent long-term goals that you set?

What are the three long-term goals that you have focused on that you are bringing into reality? Again, I'm not talking about the fantasies that nothing is happening with. I want the dreams you are bringing into reality slowly but surely, the dreams that have been dominating your mind and your thoughts for a time – the dreams that you are bringing into daily life, step by step by step.

What are the three most consistent long-term goals that you have set?

_____
_____
_____
_____

13. What do you love to learn and read about most?

What are the three most common topics you love learning or reading about most? What three topics can you stay focused on and love learning about without distraction.

What are the three things you love to learn and read about?

_____
_____
_____
_____

Step Two:
Identify the Answers That Repeat Most Often

Once you've written down three answers for each of the 13 questions, you'll see that among your 39 answers, there is a certain amount of repetition – perhaps even a lot of repetition. You may be expressing the same kinds of value in different ways – for example, "spending time with people I like," "having a drink with the folks from work," "going out to eat with my friends" – but if you look closely, you can see some patterns begin to emerge.

So look at the answer that is most often repeated and write beside it the number of how often it repeats. Then find the second most frequent answer, then the third, and so on, until you have ranked every single answer.

This gives you a good primary indicator of what your highest values are.

You can even start making decisions based on this initial hierarchy of values – and you can see how your life is already demonstrating your commitment to these values.

> "The space and time in your innermost dominant thought determines your outermost tangible reality"
> – Dr John Demartini

THE MYERS-BRIGGS PERSONALITY TYPE INDICATOR

The MBti, a model for assessing people's personalities, defines 16 different personality types, driven from the combination of four main personality types.

While knowing your MBti type probably won't help you know EVERYTHING about yourself, it can help you dig deep and get behind who you are and discover a lot about yourself.

It's one of the most accurate and popular personality theories out there.

There are four main letters involved in the MBti, based on four different personality traits. They are:

E or I – Extroversion and Introversion

This is the first of the four traits. An extrovert is someone who charges on being around other people, they get energized from spending time with others, while an introvert is someone who thrives on alone time to recharge his or her energy levels. Introverts may be less talkative, a little more reserved, because essentially, they live in their internal environment, while extroverts are more connected to the external environment, so they connect more with others.

S or N – Sensing and Intuition

Some people will use their senses to collect info from the external world, while others use their intuition to get them the information they want.

T or F – Thinking and Feeling

Thinkers use their minds to make decisions and analyze situations, without giving too much thought to their emotions in decision making. Feelers use mainly their emotions in the decision making process, giving less thought to the logic when making decisions in life.

J or P – Judging and Perceiving

Judging personalities make their own decisions in life, and they like to be in control over organizing their own lives. The perceiving personality however, doesn't put much weight to planning. These people are flexible and like to keep things simple and as they are

The 16 Different Types

If you've figured out which traits describe you most accurately, it's time to start putting them together to analyze your real personality type according to the Myers Briggs Personality Type Indicator.

Let's say for example you are a thinker (T), judging (J), sensing (S) and you're an introvert (I), your personality type is ISTJ.

There's a lot of difference between the 16 types of personalities. Here are the personality traits, each under their unique personality types:

The ISTJ Personality

These personalities are Introverted, Sensing, Thinking and Judging. They collect information based on their senses and then take logical decisions based on practical facts. This personality is not a procrastinator and knows how to get the job done.

Common traits include:
Organized and uses logic in thinking and judging scenarios
Hard working, achiever and self-motivated
Target driven and won't stop until the goal is attained
Very dependable and loyal
May be subject to more stress due to strong commitment to achieving goals
Perfect planner, goal oriented and hard worker that always aims to achieve

The ISTJ and Relationships
ISTJ types get along great with other introverts, but due to the difference in their nature, ISTJ personalities have a hard time getting into relationships with extroverted people. Due to his goal focused personality, the ISTJ personality might seem a little harsh at times, which could lead to problems in relationships.

The ESTJ Personality
This is an Extroverted, Sensing, Thinking and Judging personality. It's an extrovert who collects information based on his senses and makes decisions based on logic and facts. He's a great planner who likes to take control of his own life.

Common Traits Include:
Confidence, problem solver and puts information into practice
Can be a little aggressive towards others who don't accept their ideas
Very practical
Have natural leadership abilities, obviously likes to be in charge
Goal oriented, rarely leaves tasks unfinished
Likes logic and logical judgments, feelings rarely dominate his decisions
May become subject to stress due to his strong commitment to achieving his goals

The ESTJ and Relationships
The ESTJ personality can be very practical, to such an extent that it might annoy his partner. Conflicts might arise in relationships unless the ESTJ type personality partners up with another practical person. The ESTJ personality has great planning abilities, which can help them save relationships and keep them going.

The ISTP Personality
This is an Introverted, Sensing, Thinking, Perceiving personality. The ISTP collects information based on his sense and uses logic to make decisions. They are good planners, but might not have as much control over their own lives as the ISTJ personalities.

Common Traits Include:
Interested in facts and makes decisions that are based on logic
He likes to be alone to process the happenings in life
Likely to rather make decisions based on solid data than on his emotions
Great personalities for technical jobs
Tend to live in their own internal world

The ISTP and Relationships
The best partner for an ISTP would be another introvert because he needs his own space more often than not. The ISTP personality might seem a little harsh at times due to his decision making logic.

The ISFJ Personality
This is an Introverted, Sensing, Feeling and Judging personality. This personality does love the company of others, although he prefers to stay alone. They collect information based on their sense and use their feelings to make decisions, which is why they are more people oriented than the ISTP personality types. They have good planning skills and have no problems with setting and achieving goals.

Common Traits Include:
Collects data by logic but acts based on their feelings
Depends on feelings for taking action, which is why they are usually kind people
Usually is a nurturing partner and protector who protects others from harm
Usually tend to be a little reserved
Very responsible and reliable
Hard working
Might focus so much on the needs of others that they forget about their own needs

The ISFJ and Relationships
The ISFJ is most compatible with another introvert. They are kind and passionate, which is why being in a relationship with ISFJ personalities feels so comfortable.

The ISFP Personality
This is an Introverted, Sensing, Feeling and Perceiving personality type. They collect data based on their senses and make decisions based on their feelings, which is why they have empathy for others. They aren't good planners and can have serious issues with goal setting and achieving.

Common Traits Include:
Introverted by nature, tends to quit projects mid-way and rarely share their emotions with others
Artistic by nature, appreciates the art
May set very high standards for themselves or be perfectionistic
May be sensitive, which is why they have empathy for others
They dislike rules and rigid systems due to their artistic nature

The ISFP and Relationships
The ISFP make a great relationship partners, due to their kindness and empathy, although their lack of planning abilities might cause troubles in their relationships. Their kind nature however makes their partners overlook the planning problem issue.

The INFJ Personality
These are Introverted, Intuitive, Feeling, and Judging personalities. They collect information based on intuition and make decisions based on their feelings and their value system.

Common Traits Include:
They use feelings to act on their intuition
They follow their intuition and give less weight to logic and solid facts
They are subject to depression because they only have a few close friends and don't often share their thoughts and emotions with others
Can be oversensitive and easily hurt
Tend to be a little perfectionistic that could actually harm their self-esteem
They'll avoid tasks that involve complex details unless they really have to do them
Creative and artistic

The INFJ and Relationships
INFJ personalities do their best to make relationships work and last, but they can be a little uncomfortable to deal with, due to their lack of interest about details. They are warm and caring people, who are loving and make for great relationship partners.

The ESFJ Personality Type

These are Extroverted, Sensing, Feeling and Judging personalities. They love people and social life. They collect information based on their senses rather than their intuition and then make decisions based on their feelings. ESFJ are doers, they are goal oriented and can set and follow through goals.

Common Traits Include:
Organizes information using logic and then use their feelings to act
Social by nature
They understand people's emotions and feelings so they are compassionate
They might tend to be a little over sensitive sometimes
They are people pleasers
They tend to be concerned about social approval

The ESFJ and Relationships
ESFJ personalities care a lot about others which is why they usually have very successful relationships. Because they are goal oriented and compassionate, they usually set goals of pleasing their partner, and more often than not, succeed.

The ENFP Personality

These personalities are Extroverted, Intuitive, Feeling and Perceiving. They collect information externally and then use their feelings to make decisions. The way they feel determines their actions to a great extent, and they are fast decision makers. They are self-motivated and optimistic, thus inspire others with these traits.

Common Traits Include:
Can make decisions because they "feel" right, and aren't necessarily backed by solid information
Hates detailed tasks
Prefer to use their creativity to solve problems
These personalities like to explore and discover new possibilities
Tend to be adventurous lovers
Tend to be risk takers

They focus more on the future than on the present moment
They are optimistic

The ENFP and Relationships:
Because ENFP personalities are warm, they usually have healthy relationships. They also always take feelings into account which is why they are kind and nurturing partners.

The INTP Personality
INTP personalities are Introverted, Intuitive, Thinking and Perceiving. They collect information through intuition and make decisions based on logic and rationality.

Common Traits Include:
They are analyzers and organize information in logical ways
They are interested in technical aspects
They usually have a deep love for reading
They are introverted by nature, spending a lot of time in their internal worlds
They are very intellectual
They might be a little over sensitive at times and tend to be a little shy

The INTP and Relationships:
INTP personalities take a lot of time to analyze new people and take a long time to open up to others. Once they feel comfortable, INTP personalities can be great relationship partners.

The INTJ Personality
These are Introverted, Intuitive, Thinking and Judging personalities. They are goal oriented and know how to get tasks done. They collect information based on their intuition and use logic to make decisions.

Common Traits Include:
They use their logic to take action
With their introverted intuition, they use intuition to deal with their inner thoughts and emotions.
They have figure orientation, and focus more on the future, than the present moment

They love to plan, set goals and follow strategies
They set very high standards for themselves, and tend to be a little perfectionistic
They are big picture oriented
Likes and values knowledge
They are ambitious
They are creative

<u>The INTJ and Relationships:</u>
INTJ personalities might face problems in their relationships because they tend to forget about other people's feelings when making decisions. They prefer quiet space and would do great in a relationship with another introverted personality.

The ESTP Personality
ESTP personalities are Extroverted, Sensing, Thinking and Perceiving. They are social people who love others. They are very logical thinkers who like to analyze everything and want to understand everything in detail. Because they use logic to think and act, they might come across as cold, not taking other's emotions into account. They are action oriented and want to get tasks done as soon as possible.

<u>Common Traits Include:</u>
They collect information with their sense and use logic to take action
They focus more on the present moment than the future
They are action oriented
They are risk takers
They are highly energetic
They focus on practical ideas and love to deal with solid facts
They can be flexible, but also blunt at times
They love to plan and take action

<u>The ESTP and Relationships:</u>
Due to their can-do attitude, ESTP personalities are attractive and charming. Their way of taking action can be a little harsh for feelers who make decisions based on feelings. ESTP personalities usually see

their relationships as tasks that have to be done properly, which is why they usually have very successful relationships.

The INFP Personality
INFP personalities are Introverted, Intuitive, Feeling and Perceiving. They collect information by intuition and make decisions based on their feelings. They are very kind, caring and warm people. They are also idealistic, which sometimes leads them to be a little perfectionistic.

Common Traits Include:
They take action based on their feelings
They are compassionate
They have high inner values
They tend to be a little perfectionistic
They understand others well and try to please others
They are future oriented
They are very creative and artistic
They tend to be a little over sensitive
They enjoy the company of others even though they are introverted

The INFP and Relationships:
Their lack of interest in minor details makes INFP personalities easy to deal with and their compassion makes them easy to love. They would do well in a relationship where the other partner is equally idealistic.

The ESFP Personality
ESFP personalities are Extroverted, Sensing, Feeling and Perceiving. They are outgoing and collect information with their external senses. They are also feelers so they depend on their emotions for decision making, which makes them more people oriented

Common Traits Include:
Emotional decision makers
More focused on the present moment than the future
The give a lot of weight to facts and practical methods

Warm and compassionate
They love to be the center of attention
Have a deep love for life itself
Very social
Takes random decisions and rarely has set plans

The ESFP and Relationships:
ESFP personalities are usually very successful at maintaining long term relationships because of their warmth, love for others and because they tend to put other people's emotional needs before their own.

The ENTP Personality
These personalities are Extroverted, Intuitive, Thinking and Perceiving. The collect information based on their intuition and use logic when it comes to making decisions. They are deep thinkers and can be slow at making decisions.

Common Traits Include:
Logical decision maker
More focused on the future than the present moment
They love exploring and trying new things
They tend to understand their environment very well
Some ENTP personalities are very creative
They aren't the most goal oriented people around
They tend to ignore the emotions and feelings of others
Flexible and very social
Problem solvers

The ENTP and Relationships:
Because ENTP's aren't goal oriented, they might delay tasks and forget about them, which make them appear to be irresponsible. The ENTP personality does great with a partner that understands his way of thinking and shares a common way of thinking and logical reasoning.

The ENFJ Personality
ENFJ personalities are Extroverted, Intuitive, Feeling and Judging. They easily set and achieve goals. They also take other people's feelings into consideration whenever making decisions. They collect information by means of their intuition.

Common Traits Include:
Decision making relies heavily on the emotions of others for ENFJ personalities
Compassionate
Can be over sensitive
They love being around people and have deep understanding for social relationships
They love to help others
Warm and charming
Creative

The ENFJ and Relationships:
ENFJ personalities usually have great love and family relationships. Because they are so warm, compassionate and understanding, they are always weary of hurting others' feelings, which is why people love to be around them.

The ENTJ Personality
ENTJ's are Extroverted, Intuitive, Thinking and Judging. They collect information based on intuition and use logic to make decisions.

Common Traits Include:
Logical thinker
Very social
Tend to be a bit critical
Have natural leadership abilities and powerful decision making skills
More focused on the future than the present moment
Not someone who dwells on past mistakes
Very self-confident
Decisive

<u>The ENTJ and Relationships:</u>
ENTJ personalities always strive to improve their relationships with logic reasoning. They take charge in relationships, but their critical nature could become problematic.

The Fear of Success Scale

This test is designed to indicate how fearful you are of achieving success in life, be it consciously or subconsciously.

It gives you an indication of why you might not be achieving your goals and indicates whether or not you're limiting yourself for achieving success in life.
This will also indicate just how driven you are and what drive you have to accomplish your set goals and objectives.

Answer the following questions with either a T or an F. If the answer is mostly true, answer with a T. If the answer is mostly false, answer with an F.

1. Sometimes I'm afraid to do things as well as I know I could.

2. I am prone to worry about the possibility of being disliked by others for doing well at something.

3. I never worry about the possibility of being disliked by others for doing well at something.

4. I sometimes do less than my very best so that no one will be threatened.

5. I often worry about the possibility that others may think I work too hard.

6. I never worry about the possibility that others may think I work too hard.

7. I would find it nerve-wracking to be regarded as one of the best in my field.

8. I seem to be more anxious after succeeding at something than after failing at something.

9. I would worry that others might think I was peculiar or strange if I were too devoted to my work.

10. I have occasionally deliberately done average or mediocre work in order to make sure that someone else would do it better than me.

11. I sometimes worry that others will expect too much of me.

12. I usually set goals for myself that are lower than what I am capable of reaching.

13. I seem to be drawn to activities that are not very challenging.

14. I do not enjoy doing superior work as much as I feel that I should.

15. I do not like competing with others if there is a possibility that hard feelings towards me may develop.

16. I worry about the possibility of being criticized by my friends or associates for being too involved with my own work.

17. I sometimes worry that I may become too well informed for my own good.

18. I never worry about the possibility that friendships may have to be sacrificed in order to accomplish certain tasks or kinds of work.

19. If I were outstanding at something, I would worry about the possibility of others making fun of me behind my back.

20. I do not worry about the personal feelings of others when it comes to getting something important done.

21. I have a tendency to worry that someone might become jealous if I do too well at something.

22. I would never worry about the possibility that academic or occupational success might interfere with success in social relationships.

23. I would never worry about the possibility that others might feel uncomfortable or ill at ease around me if I were too competent at something.

24. I have a fear that others might like me only for what I could do for them due to my competency in a certain field.

25. I am prone to worry that undue pressures would be placed on me if I were to develop considerable competency in some field.

26. I worry that I may become so knowledgeable that others will not like me.

27. I would worry that others might try to take advantage of me if I were extremely competent at something.

28. If I were to do well at something, I would worry that someone might try to undermine my success.

29. I would worry that others might be afraid of me if they felt that I understood people too well.

SCORING KEY

If you answered most of your answers with a T, you have an inherent fear of succeeding in life. If you answered most of your answers with an F, you have a passionate drive to succeed in life.

CHAPTER 9

How to Increase Your Self-Esteem

As far as your self-esteem is concerned, the only opinion that really matters is **your own**. And even then, you should be evaluating that opinion very *carefully* since we all tend to be our own harshest critics.

When you have healthy self-esteem, you have a realistic, appreciative opinion of yourself. Unconditional human worth assumes that we're all born with all the capabilities we need to live fruitfully, although everyone has a different mix of skills, which are at different levels of development.

Some of us navigate this life - *and our relationships* - searching for the tiniest amount of evidence to validate our self-limiting beliefs. Just like with a judge and jury, we're constantly putting ourselves on trial, and sometimes, sentence ourselves to a lifetime of self-criticism.

The time has come for you to break that cycle, to step up to the plate, break down any limiting beliefs, and just start loving yourself and your life again.

Here are some amazing tips to help you build your self-esteem and self-love:

1. Be mindful.
If we don't admit that there's something that has to change, we'll never be able to fix a problem. By becoming aware of your negative self-talk, you can begin to distance yourself from the feelings it brings it. Without that awareness, it's easy to fall into the trap of believing the self-limiting conversations we have with ourselves on a regular basis. The trick here is not to believe everything you think. Thoughts are just that - thoughts - not facts.

2. Change the story.
You probably have a narrative or backstory you've created for yourself, the one that shapes your self-perception, the one upon which your self-image is based. In order to change that story, you have to understand where it came from and where you received the messages you're playing to yourself over and over again. Whose voice are you internalizing?

It's not uncommon for automatic negative thoughts like "You're fat!" or "You're lazy!" to get repeated in your mind, and if they're repeated often enough, you can bet your butt they're going to stick, and pretty soon you'll believe them to be true.

You see, this negative self-talk is learned, which also means that it can be unlearned. Start with positive affirmations. Is there something you wish you believed about yourself? Write down those phrases and then repeat them to yourself every day.

3. Don't fall into the compare-and-despair trap.
Practicing acceptance and not comparing yourself to others is key to successfully building your self-esteem. Just because someone you know looks happy on social media doesn't necessarily mean that they are. Comparing yourself to a false image that someone might be portraying can only lead to negative self-talk, which then leads to stress and anxiety.

4. Find your inner glow.
Albert Einstein said: "Everybody is a genius, but if you judge a fish by its ability to climb a tree, it will live its whole life believing that it is

stupid." You have your weaknesses, but you also have amazing strengths. You might be amazing with adventure sports, but less-than-amazing at dancing and neither quality defines your core worth. When you focus on your strengths, you get to focus on the feeling of confidence that those strengths engender.

5. Remember that you are not your circumstances.
When you learn how to differentiate between your circumstances and who you truly are, you'll have a recipe for success as far as building self-worth goes. Recognize that you have your own, unique inner world and that even though you might have some imperfections, you should love yourself for them as well.

6. Challenge yourself.
Sit down and make a list of things you find difficult, hard, or even impossible to do…and then go out and DO them. Self-esteem is built when you're doing something you imagine to be hard or impossible. If you live life doing easy things, life will become hard, but if you live your life doing one hard thing after the other, life will become easy.

7. Take a look in the mirror.
Look at yourself in the mirror and say: "I love you. I love you. I love you!" until you have tears streaming down your face. It's a powerful experience, and everyone has to try it at least once in their life. It's one of the best ways to break down the external walls you've erected over the years and just get real with your inner self.

8. Forgive yourself.
You have always done the best you could, with the resources that you had available, and you are still always doing the best you can, with the resources you now have available. No matter what you've done (or haven't done), you are worthy of love. I would recommend using something like the 'Golden Altar of Forgiveness' exercise by Stewart Swerdlow.

9. Take good care of your body.
When you have a healthy body, it paves the way to a healthy mindset, which is what you need in order to build self-love. I like to take care of

my body by starting the day with a glass of water. I also alkalize my body with a green smoothie and then have a piece of fruit, just to jump-start my metabolism. Although I'm not super strict with my diet, I do eat in moderation and practice mindful eating where I focus on what I eat and how it's nurturing my body.

Remember that developing better self-esteem requires you to be more proactive in life. Having positive self-esteem implies a willingness to accept total responsibility, which means that if you accept and trust yourself completely, you're freeing yourself from self-criticism, which will boost your self-love.

Even though you might not believe it, the way you behave towards others WILL have an impact on your self-esteem because when you have high self-esteem, you have respect for yourself, which allows you to have deep respect for others around you too.

Self-assured people don't only admit their imperfections, but they applaud them. The flaws in you are a part of who you are. It points out where your strengths lie, shows you where you need to improve and when to let others take the lead. Trying to be perfect at everything you do is unrealistic, the game never gets easier, you just get better at it. Love yourself for who you are and who you know you're not.

Learning Self-Love through Good Deeds

The Law of Moses says: "Do unto others as you would have them do unto you." It's a biblical thing, and I get that not everyone is going to like the idea, but there is a lot of insight to the idea. It forms part of my foundational ground rules in life, and I reckon that it has been a massive influence in my journey towards self-love.

Why?

Well, because it's about so much more than just being kind to others or doing good stuff in the world around you. I mean sure, I'd love to be assisted by someone whenever I find myself in a less-than-amazing pickle, but in my life, I try to create equality that often goes unnoticed by other people.

Reaching a point in your life where you've adjusted your attitude to align with the idea of treating others the way you'd like to be treated is such a fulfilling experience.

And it doesn't stop at physically treating others the way you'd like to be treated, it's about thinking about how you'd feel if you were in their situation as well.

You have to stop focusing on punishing those who do you an injustice, and instead, move yourself into a better frame of mind. Instead of pointing out other people's flaws (which are actually just a mirror of your own flaws), try to get them to see the flaws in their way of thinking.

Respect and Your Journey Towards Self-Love

Being respectful and courteous in your interactions with others is a great way of building self-esteem and self-love. It shouldn't be a behavior that you set aside for special occasions; it should be a way of life, even when you're just hanging out with yourself.

People who understand and show gratitude in their day to day activities are much less likely to have diminished self-esteem, are much less likely to fall victim to depression, and have a much higher sense of self-love, in general.

When I was growing up, gratitude was forced on me. I reckon it's something that we all have to be brought up with, not just something we pick up along the line.

Hand-in-hand with respect and gratitude, I'd say that having fun is one of the best ways you can foster self-love.

Happiness is your birthright, and yes, we all create our own happiness. We all have to go through bad experiences sometimes, and we have to deal with negative emotions, but in trying to always lead a happy life, we have to accept our pasts, embrace it, learn from it, and then move on.

Our emotions are based on how we think, how we perceive the present moment, and of course, our internal dialogue plays a massive role. All of us are emotional beings, but by letting negative emotions rule us, we're dooming out fate.

When something bad has happened in your life, you can't change the outcome, but you can change where you go from there with what you have learned from the situation.

Not everything in life will go according to your plan. Not everything will bring a smile to your dial. But there is ALWAYS something positive to focus on.

Sadness is NOT your destiny. Not loving yourself enough is NOT your destiny. You are NOT a victim of negativity.

You've probably been through your fair share of ups and downs throughout the course of your life, but you have the option of CHOOSING to LOVE LIFE and living it fully, every, single, day. The happier you are as a person, the less likely you'll be to fall victim to negative thoughts and events.

I believe that when you're truly loving life and being happy, you'll have no other choice than to feel warm and fuzzy inside. Surrounding yourself with people whom you love and who are there to support you will only enrich your life and make you a happier person as a whole.

People who are the most loving and the most giving, people who do good things without expecting anything in return, those are the happiest people you will ever meet in your life.

In her book *Bringers of the Dawn*, Barbara Marciniak says:

> *"Laughter is very sweet and good. Have a cosmic laugh at the irony of things. Laughter relaxes the chakras...*
>
> *Some people have cured themselves of cancer by watching funny movies. They laugh themselves into healing.... Cancer comes from anger. It comes from pollutants, toxicity...but all the poisons in the world cannot really 'land' in you unless you create the emotional trauma to house it. And cancer is a seat of anger, a seat of 'I've been wronged,' 'I've been screwed,' 'I've been traumatized,' 'I've been betrayed'...*
>
> *This happens on a deep-feeling level. The cells in the body are the ones that REALLY know you. You can trick the pea, but you can't trick the body. So <u>LAUGHTER is a sign of an elevated spirit. Laughter heals the body and opens up the chakras to take healing energy inside</u>."*

Every single day, we all have a choice to grieve, feel sorry for ourselves, and contemplate whether or not we could have done things differently. The answer is no. Life is life, and you have no control over what others do. Instead, you can focus on what you can do to the best of your abilities.

Nothing in this world can bring life back or change something that has already occurred. I believe that I am the driver of my own happiness, and so are you. Do not simply accept to be the passenger in this vehicle, take control, and get behind the steering wheel of your gateway to happiness!

As with all things in life, practice makes perfect, so do your best at trying to be happy and focusing on loving yourself with your efforts. Be thankful and grateful for each new day and the abundance of possibilities it brings. At the very least, just be grateful for the air you get to breathe into your lungs every single day, so many people no longer have that privilege, remember that!

How to Build Your Dream Outcome

Building self-esteem and learning to love yourself and your life again requires having a dream. In order to create a life where you're self-confident, you'll have to set some serious goals so that you're able to build an outcome that you're happy with.

Want to know a secret? Confident people KNOW what they want. They are goal-oriented.

Goals work because thoughts are things. Everything you see around you started out as something in someone's imagination. Someone imagined designing and building a telephone, a light bulb, an air-conditioning system. And it all turned into realities. Whatever you imagine and focus on and move towards, can be created and manifested, and brought to life within your world.

When you focus your mind on your goals and your dream outcome, you're acknowledging to your conscious and subconscious mind that where you are right now, is not where you want to be, that you have bigger plans for this life, and that you're working hard to get there.

Dissatisfaction can be a tool which you can use to help you achieve your goals. You see, as part of what motivated human behavior, action is a sense of dissatisfaction, and without a certain amount of pressure, there simply isn't any motivation to get things done.

When you create a compelling goal for your life, you'll have the ability to jump out of bed each morning with an amazing drive and heaps of energy. What drives people is a compelling goal, the thought of a future that excites and gets them going.

So here's how to work on and achieve your goals: KNOW what you want. WRITE YOUR GOALS DOWN. There's nothing quite as powerful as having clarity over what it is you want.

Our brains are constantly scanning and filtering, deleting 99.9% of everything we perceive. Why? Because we'd all be bonkers from information overload if it didn't.

You see, our Reticular Activating Systems (RAS) bring to our attention if something seems 0.01% important. The best way to get your RAS to work for you in an empowering way is to set and write down your goals.

When you write your goals down, you're sending a clear order to your brain that **"Hey. This is important. This is what I want, now get it for me!"**

Integrity demands that we get straight with ourselves. Sometimes it's the toughest thing you'll ever have to do, but it's also the foundation of a joyous life. It's the key to self-expression and power. It's the key to everything related to success.

The foundation of self-confidence is LIVING IN ACCORDANCE with your values.

As long as you're doing the right thing, the world can literally collapse around you, and you'll maintain peace of mind, stay cool, and be as confident as ever.

Integrity is VITAL to high self-confidence. It is an essential value to have, and it is more than just a value, it ensures that all your other values are respected and lived in line with. You can't have just a little bit of integrity. You can't put integrity aside when it's not convenient.

From the moment you've selected your core values, you can never compromise them. This is the measure of your quality as a human being. As long as you know, deep down inside of you, that you'll never violate your highest value (which is integrity), you'll be in total control and full of self-confidence and self-love.

The Bigger Picture - How to Completely Take Charge of Your Self-Esteem

You've already read through A LOT of information in this book, but let me tell you: for me, it all comes down to points of power that will help you completely transform your life and regain your self-love and build your self-esteem. It looks like this:

1. Play it BIG. Take charge of your dreams and enjoy the ride.
Listen, you're going to die anyway, so you might as well go for it and have a blast.
Be a player in this game called life. Play full out. Be fully alive. Take advantage of every moment you are given! Live a BIG life. Create a big game, where you are challenged every moment to be at your very best.

Life is NOT a movie. You only get ONE take, so make it work for you in all the right ways.

"Someone should tell us, right at the start of our lives that we're dying. Then, we might live life to the limit! Every minute of every day! DO IT, I SAY! WHATEVER IT IS YO WANT TO DO! Do it NOW! There are only so many tomorrows..."
- Actor Michael Landon

Is there something that you REALLY like doing, something that gets you fired up, and something you want to create? Remember that anything you can conceive, you can achieve!

2. Help others. And do so often.
Taking action is one of the best things you can ever do to achieve self-confidence, but the second most important thing you have to do is to help others achieve what they want.

Is there a way in which you can add value to the life of somebody else? How can you care for other people? Who out there could use a helping hand from you?

When we focus too much on ourselves and forget about the needs of those around us, we're creating surefire pitfalls for self-confidence and self-love. When we can focus on helping others and contribute to their lives, we're living beyond just our own existence, and we're partaking in life on a much grander scale.

Focusing on giving allows us to become more spiritual. Giving our time, our attention, our love, allows us to recognize what we were truly designed for. It gets us to that point where we're finally able to realize that we are here to give, and not just to get.

The universe always rewards those that are living their lives in line with their true purpose, those who are serving others. And here's the great thing: the more you serve others, the more you receive it back!

Instead of focusing on *"What's in it for me?"* try shifting your focus *to "How can I serve more people?"* because it will help you live a life with purpose and help you shift your quality of life.

3. Stop working yourself to death and start living your purpose!

If you're stuck in a dead-end job, working in a field you hate just to make ends meet; you're never going to feel fulfilled. You might make it to the top of the corporate ladder in ten or twenty years from now, but you would have wasted your precious life doing something you have ZERO passion for.

Get out there and find something that excites you, that drives you, that makes you feel like you're doing great and making a difference in the world, and then LIVE IT. When you're living and breathing your true purpose, it's not hard work, that's called being fully alive!

4. Get into the flow of life.

Being in the flow of life means being passionate about what you do, being excited about the future, being driven, motivated, successful, enthusiastic, loyal, faithful, creative, self-expressed, it's about being fully alive in everything you do. It's about feeling like you're on the right track, inviting the right people and situations into your life.

There IS a possibility out there that wants YOU. There is a mission out there that's powerfully calling you! You just have to discover it and then give your life to it. Go into it with your whole heart, your whole soul, your whole being!

Yes, it requires courage, integrity, and passion, but just get out there and TAKE A STAND for what you BELIEVE in.

I promise you this: You'll never wish you'd spent more time at the office when you're lying on your death bed!

Do what YOU love in life. Close your eyes and just picture yourself living your ideal life, doing your ideal job. Can you see it? What are you doing?

DO NOT settle for where you are if it is incongruent with what you really want to be doing.

5. Use spiritual enlightenment to gain self-confidence

Lee Carroll, the author of a series of books on spiritual enlightenment, uses her life to channel a spiritual entity called "Kryon." Kryon claims that he is one of the many spiritual entities that are of service to mankind, doing the work of God, from the other side of the veil.

According to the books, Kryon goes on to say that humans are spiritual beings that are here for the human experience. We're all in 'lesson' in the 'school' called earth. We're here to learn about the purpose of growing our awareness and thus, to raise our vibration, we have to get more and more enlightened through expressions of love, peace, and tolerance. It also explains that we are all part of the God; we are all part of the same consciousness.

While I'm not advocating nor denying these claims, I do suspect that there might be some truth to it. If we're all part of the same consciousness, it surely means that the only feeling we should be experiencing is LOVE.

Love for those around us. Love for the world we call home. Love for the beauty of nature. And of course, love for ourselves.

I strongly believe that we're all here for a reason and that we're all much more important than we give ourselves credit for. But what does this mean for self-confidence, self-love, and self-esteem?

Let me tell you this: there is a timeless place inside of you that has unlimited and eternal love, which can be tapped into at any given time. We all have to nurture that gift so that we have more to give.

Whenever we love, we'll feel loved in return. Whenever we cherish, we'll feel cherished in return. Whenever we value life, we'll feel like life values us in return, whenever we value nature, we'll feel like nature values us in return. Anytime we express any kind of love, we'll feel it in return, and THAT is the one true answer to building self-love and self-confidence.

Building Self-Esteem with Authenticity

Who are you?

At your core, who are you really?

It's a question so often asked that there has to be a plausible answer, a black-and-white answer, right?

Identity struggles can be very hard to overcome, and trying to build up healthy self-esteem and self-love can be impossible to do if you don't even know who you are.

But there's a lot of irony in the question, because the more you battle with identifying yourself, the more you change, and the more the OLD you diminishes.

Discovering who you are should not be the emphasis. Instead, you should be facilitating the emergence of YOU would like to experience.

In essence, identity is an **ongoing** process. It's not just a quick snapshot, which means that we should actually be focusing on reframing, rethinking and reconsidering ourselves perpetually as part of our life's journey.

A lot of people tend to feel *inadequate*, which is why they ponder the thought of who they really are. But there's a beautiful thing that happens once you discover that your efforts should be attuned to the unfolding of your life when you start being the change you wish to see in your world.

People, who *'claim'* to know themselves extremely well, are in fact expressing their fragility in identity. Why? Because when you know yourself SO well, there's simply NO ROOM for personal growth. It could be that they don't think they have any growing to do, or simply be an indicator that they are too scared of personal growth that they fear the eventual outcomes of a deeper level of self-discovery.

Becoming *intimately aware* of our thoughts, our feelings, our hopes, and our fears is always a good idea, and always makes sense, regardless of where you find yourself in life.

Because the universe exists in a state of flowing potential, it also means that the inner self should be open to new potential, to growth, at any point. Because we're part of the universe that's always changing, we should also be in a constant state of flowing potential.

The process of introspection is called positive disintegration. We access potential, keeping the parts of the self that serve us, and getting rid or what burdens and constrains us. When you do this on a regular basis, you're allowing yourself to find the perfect balance between extremes, and you're entering into a real, blissful relationship with the self, committing to your personal evolution!

The Importance of Being True to Yourself
When you first entered this world, it was with a blank slate and a clear mind. You were open to the most subtle impressions.

As you grew up, you were continuously building your defenses, coming up with new limiting beliefs, working on your ego, and perhaps, even getting down with some self-harm in the process.

Now you have an idea of who you think you are.

But you also know that you're not going to live forever. So you begin to challenge that perception of who you thought you were. You start wondering why you're here and you ponder the idea of where it is you're heading with your life.

Are you really living life on your terms, or are you leading a life where you're always doing what's expected of you?

If you don't KNOW who you are - or at least what you stand for - you'll never be able to answer those questions authentically.

Let's see how well you know yourself:
What unique talents, skills, or gifts do you have?
Are there any life challenges that are getting in the way of where it is you want to go with your life?
Does your personality have control over your life, and if so, to what extent?
Does your soul inspire and drive you?
What is it that gives your life purpose and meaning?

Don't worry if you can't give definitive answers to those questions; the truth is that you're NOT alone. Most people in life struggle with answering those questions.

Before you can answer those questions, you'll have to shift your fear of the unknown aside and delve even deeper into your journey of self-discovery!

Authenticity and Self-Love Go Hand-in-Hand

Have you ever noticed the expression on a little kid's face when he sees himself in a mirror for the first time? That first reflection is an affliction and a revelation in one single shot.

You see infants have no capacity for self-awareness. When they reach the age of two years old, they start becoming more conscious of their own thoughts, their feelings, and the sensations they feel with every interaction they have in this life. That's also around the time they'll start embarking on a quest that will consume the rest of their lives for the most part.

As humans, our hunger for authenticity guides us at every age and every aspect of our personal development. Authenticity is what drives us to do the kind of jobs we end up doing one day, what fuels our relationships, what makes us play, and what spikes our interest in areas such as politics and religion.

Authenticity defines our fashions, or hobbies, our friends, our lovers, our jobs, our locations, and our living arrangements. Authenticity is what helps us define what 'fits' and what 'isn't our scene.'

Then there's something else you have to keep in mind: we live in a fake world. The world has become so used to lies that it is now offended by the truth. With the likes of cosmetic surgery, psychopharmaceuticals, and makeovers, everything seems to be contributing to the mockery that there's really nothing solid about being true to the self. Amid a clutter of counterfeits, the core self-struggles to assert itself.

"It's some kind of epidemic right now; people feel profoundly like they're not living from who they really are, their authentic self, their deepest possibility in the world. The result is a sense of near-desperation."
- Stephen Cope, author of Yoga and the Quest for the True Self

Understanding Authenticity

When we talk about authenticity, we're referring to the unimpeded operation of one's true or core self in one's daily enterprise. Well, at least that's what the dictionary says, but it's not clear what it comes down to, right?

Authenticity has four concrete cornerstones, and they look like this:

Self-Awareness

This is when you know yourself and trust in your own emotions, your motives, your preferences and your abilities.

Strengths and Weaknesses

This is about acknowledging when you're great or terrible at something, and not resorting to denial or blame.

Behavior

This is about how you act in ways that are congruent with your core values and your needs.

Honesty

Well, you know what honesty is all about - complete and total openness.

It can seem impossible to live a life that's true to one's inner self, and authenticity is becoming more and more of a phenomenon these days than it is a core value.

Aristotle connected the fruits of self-reflection with a theory that authentic behavior wasn't so much about letting your freak flag fly high, but more about acting in accord with the higher good.

But then, at the dawn of the 20th century, existentialists questioned Aristotle's idea of the true self, residing within. They perceived the self to be something that was made, rather than born, and that the choice of your actions was responsible for the creation of self, and as such, of authenticity.

Now psychologists believe that authenticity, and in essence, the self, is an array of conflicting impressions, sensations, and behaviors.

Our heads are much messier than previously thought, and we're dooming our sense of authenticity with our attempts of tidying up the sense of self, restricting our identities to what we 'want' to be or who we 'think' we ought to be.

For a lot of people, modern day life has made it nearly impossible to be authentic. The simple truth is that self-knowledge can be one of the most painful things because it's not always fun to discover the deeper, somewhat darker things about yourself. And aside from just discovering them, once you know they exist, you'll have to accept and live with them.

A lot of people also find it hard to be authentic because they fear rejection. For some, it's easier to lead fake lives and be accepted than to be true to themselves and risked being kicked to the curb by society, all just because you were being the real you.

By leading an authentic life, true to the real self, you have to be willing to make conscious, informed choices about your self-knowledge. You'll have to be willing to evaluate everything you do.

Authenticity demands psychological exertion that depletes the self's executive function. Being authentic takes a LOT more work and is MUCH easier said than done.

When we lead authentic lives, we're accepting contradiction, discomfort, personal faults, and failures. Whenever we experience failure, it's not due to breaches of the true self, but rather clues to the more comprehensive mystery that is selfhood, self-love, and self-esteem.

"Not until we are lost do we truly begin to find ourselves." - **Henry David Thoreau**

Exercise

In order to help raise your self-confidence levels, I'm going to need you to pull out your journal again. Grab a pen, and then as soon as you're ready, start working on this exercise…

1. List ten things you love about yourself.

2. What are your ten best skills?

3. What are five achievements you're really proud of?

4. List three occasions where you have overcome adversity.

5. If you only had six months left to live, what would you spend your time doing? What's really important to you? What story do you want to leave behind?

6. Is there a specific knowledge or skill that you'd love to acquire?

Once you've answered these questions, you'll have a clear indication of what you currently love about your life and how you've already overcome hard times. You'll also have an idea of what it is you'd love even more, in terms of spending your time the way you'd want to.

Let me tell you this: If you have a desire to achieve something, you've already got the ability within you to achieve those desires. If you can believe it, you can achieve it. End of story!

You CAN create healthy self-esteem and you CAN learn to love yourself and your life again, you just need to focus your attention in the right direction!

CHAPTER 10

Meditating Your Way to Healthy Self-Esteem

The Basics of Transcendental Meditation

TM, which was founded by Maharishi Mahesh Yogi, has seen over 6 million people from across the globe learning this practice. There have been more than 350 published research studies that confirm the benefits of Transcendental Meditation and one of the most important factors about it is the fact that it can significantly improve your self-esteem and self-love.

It's a simple, natural and effortless technique that is practiced two times a day for 20 minutes at a time. It is taught by qualified instructors over a period of 4 days, using a simple 7 step program. If you would like to learn this technique, then head on over to www.tmhome.com where you'll be able to sign up for a course in TM.

It is practiced in a comfortable sitting position with your eyes closed, and it's definitely not a religion, a philosophy or a lifestyle, it's merely a practice that will offer you a state of mindfulness.

During a Transcendental Meditation session, there's an increase of Alpha Wave coherence - wakeful relaxation - and Beta Wave coherence - activity - in the brain. When the coherence in the brain is increased, it strengthens the communication between the brain's prefrontal cortex and the different areas of the brain.

Whether you're aware of it or not, there's a deep connection between your mind and your body. Your automatic nervous system is controlled by your brain, which in turn controls your bodily functions as well as the way you feel about yourself.

When you're full of negative emotions, it has a direct impact on your health, and as you can guess, being positive and enjoying life leads to better self-image and self-esteem.

Throughout my years of trying to find different ways of boosting self-esteem and self-love, I have always circled back to meditation. Why? Because it offers us all a way of stopping our constant rush through life, it gives us the time we need to focus on who we are and what we're here to do.

Benefits of Meditation

I'm sure there are a thousand brilliant benefits of meditating, but for me, these are the main perks:

It boosts your mood.
When you meditate, the pituitary gland in your brain secretes endorphins, which are beneficial to help lift your mood. These hormones also have a positive effect on your whole body.

It destroys stress.
Another benefit of endorphins being released is the fact that they help keep stress levels in check. When you meditate, you have the opportunity of processing your stressors in life and eliminate negative thoughts.

It helps you focus.
When you meditate on a regular basis, you learn how to discipline yourself, which in return offers you a way of staying focused in everyday life.

It improves sleep.
Slow wave sleep patterns are enhanced when you meditate on a regular basis, which can be beneficial to help ward off insomnia.

It lowers blood pressure.
Meditation might help lower blood pressure, in the long and short run, which can help you lead a healthier and happier life.

It blasts away pain.
Practicing meditation on a regular basis over a prolonged period of time can help you shift the way your brain perceives physical pain, which can help you manage pain more effectively and efficiently.

It connects you to others.
Sure, meditating is a very personal thing, but it also opens you up to better social behavior. Once your mind becomes more focused on compassionate feelings towards others, it'll help you create better and more meaningful relationships in your life.

It boosts the aura.
When you meditate often, it increases your positive energy levels, which leads to you becoming a person that's pleasant to be around.

I've found that one of the best ways to connect with the inner self on a daily basis is through the help of Transcendental Meditation, as you might have picked up by now. TM helps me put the happenings of my life into perspective, and it gets me into a state where I can be the person I want to be and focus on what I want from life.

Transcendental Meditation is a great technique you can use to lift your mood, reinforce your beliefs, and start loving your true self again.

When the Dalai Lama met with a group of Western psychotherapists, he enquired about what the most common issue with most of their patients was. In their responses, they were unified: a lack of self-esteem was what most of their patients had been experiencing in their lives. One of the world's most renowned spiritual figures struggled to understand how people could suffer under the wrath of low self-esteem, because you see, in his culture, all people are raised to be at one with their inner self, unlike our Western cultures which are pretty much toxic and sees every man fighting to discover who he really is.

Shaping motivation was the Dalai Lama's first thought upon waking up in the morning. He said that when we are vigilant about our intentions being focused in the right direction, we're able to not only extend our loving kindness and compassion to others, but also to our inner selves.

In practice, meditation can help us transform our lack of self-esteem into self-confidence, self-acceptance, and self-belief. It's a two-part solution.

The first way in which meditation helps us get rid of low self-esteem is by allowing us to meet, greet, and make friends with our inner selves. When we meditate, we have an opportunity of getting to know ourselves, accept ourselves, and embrace ourselves for who and what we are. Pretty soon it becomes evident that our doubts, our insecurities, and our fears are merely superficial and that they come between us and inner trust, dignity, and self-worth.

Secondly, once we start accepting and treating ourselves kindly, we might uncover the reasons behind our limiting beliefs that we are not good enough or that we do not deserve to be happy. We can then begin to invite kindness into that self-negation and lack of self-esteem until those uncertainties dissolve into self-love.

How Your Invisible World Creates Your Visible World
We live in a world of cause and effect. Our thoughts become our cause, and our present conditions become our effects. In order to

control our lives, our self-esteem, and our level of self-love, we MUST control our thoughts.

Your outer world is merely a reflection of your inner world, and it perfectly corresponds to your dominant patterns of thinking. The truth is that most of the time, we become what we think about most of the time. When you can change your thinking, you'll have the power to change your life.

When you are born, you enter this world with infinite potential. Nothing in nature or the universe operates by chance; everything runs on very precise and immutable laws. When you live within harmony of these laws, you'll experience being in the flow of life!

"The process of creation starts with thought – an idea, conception, visualization. Everything you see was once someone's idea. Nothing exists in your world that did not first exist as pure thought. This is true of the Universe as well. Matter will form out of pure energy. In fact, it is the only way it can form." – Neale Donald Walsh, "Conversations with God"

"See yourself enjoying the achievement of your goal. Feel like it's already done! Feel like it's yours! It will then manifest into your life." – Earl Nightingale

How to Build Self-Esteem with Meditation

If you're lacking confidence in yourself, you're twice defeated in the race of life. With confidence, you have won before you have even started!

The truth is that self-esteem is a very fragile thing.

Whether you'd like to own up to it or not, most of us need the recognition or acknowledgment of others in order to feel confident in ourselves and in our choices.

We've all experienced being put down or being undermined at one stage or another during our lives, and it's just all too easy to start losing belief in ourselves when we're being questioned or are feeling insecure.

Without a proper strategy for bolstering self-esteem, self-doubt can easily undermine our confidence and our capacity to achieve the goals we set for ourselves.

Most people see meditation as an uncomplicated way to connect with their spiritual selves, manage stress, and create a more balanced and peaceful way of leading their lives. When you practice meditation, a range of other tangible benefits are also brought to the table, including feeling emotionally stronger and more self-confident.

I'm sure you'll agree with me when I say that most of us are used to listening to and connecting with our thoughts more than we do with any other part of ourselves. So much so that it's easy to forget that there's so much more to us than just our chattering, wondering minds.

When you meditate on a regular basis, you can start to transcend that chatter and start to bridge the gap between your mind's thoughts and 'chatter silence,' which can help connect you to your inner essence.

Call it your spirit if you want to, or your soul, the higher self, or even divinity. The fact of the matter is that the more you connect with your inner core, the more you tend to live your life from a calmer, deeper perspective where you have a deep love for yourself.

A Crash-Course in Meditation

Although I'd advise starting out with some guided meditation, here's a brief explanation of how to get started with self-love meditation:

Step One - Find a peaceful and quiet location in which you can meditate.

Step Two - Get into a comfortable sitting position, either in a straight-back chair or on the floor with your legs crossed. Sit in a position that feels comfortable but allows you to keep your spine as straight as possible as it will promote the flow of Chi.

Step Three - To help distract your chattering mind, use a mantra. It can be something as simple as "Calm, space, or peace." Visualize what your mantra looks like and then focus on that image.

Step Four - Place your hands on your belly and then take three slow, deep breaths. Breathe deeply as you focus on how your belly expands and pushes out against your hands.

Step Five - This is where you have to visualize and say your mantra to yourself with every breath you inhale. Hold the breath for two seconds and then repeat your mantra as you exhale. It's really as simple as it sounds, and to get into the swing of it, you're going to want to make sure you're doing this five to ten minutes, twice a day.

When you start meditating on a regular basis, you'll naturally start paying less attention to the inner voices that might be emitting negative self-talk. With time, you'll begin to notice that your inner self-critic settles down and becomes silenced.

It is within the freedom of that silence that you'll get to live each moment of your life with heightened awareness of your true spirit, and within that space, you'll start to realize that you are valuable just as you are - not because of your actions - but because you're being the truest of self you can possibly be.

Before you know it, your confidence will start revealing itself to you, and you'll find yourself feeling more courageous and open to new ideas, willing to take bigger 'risks' in life while happily overriding any previous perceived or predicted failure.

Building Yourself Up with Positive Self-Talk

After (or before) meditating, take a few minutes to just talk to yourself positively. It works great when you imagine a 6-year old version of yourself sitting down in front of you, and you're there to give them gentle, caring words of encouragement.

Keep your statements short and simple. Say things that you can effortlessly agree with so that your subconscious mind will be more likely to accept your words without any protest.

You can try statements like:
"I am proud of myself."
"I feel clever and smart today."
"I can do whatever I focus my mind on."
"I believe in myself and my abilities."
"It's fun to be me."
"I feel confident."
"I have many gifts and talents."
"I thrive on challenges."
"I accept myself even though I sometimes make mistakes."
"I do my best."
"I believe in my dreams."

How Visualizations Can Empower You

In addition to your meditation and positive self-talk, visualizations can be very beneficial to help you dramatically increase your self-love. Here's how to make it work for you:

1. Take some time every day to just spend a few minutes seeing yourself completely strong and confident in whatever it is you do.
2. Ask yourself what it would feel like to be purposeful and strong every day.
3. Generate the confident feeling by remembering a time when you felt purposeful and strong.
4. If you can't remember ever feeling that way, pick a character from a book or a movie that embodies purpose and strength, then imagine yourself playing that role, feeling how confidence feels.

Visualizations are powerful because your mind doesn't know the difference between tangible reality and your imagined reality. It loves to practice for success, so the more often you sit down and imagine yourself feeling and acting completely confident, the easier it becomes to feel and act confident in your day to day experiences.

It's Time to Start Redefining Failure

A very common cause of low self-esteem is pervasive memories of past failures. But the problem doesn't lie in the failed attempts themselves, but rather in the way you feel about them.

In most cases, it is the self-judgments you made and the conclusions you came to that undermine your confidence and scupper your efforts to try again.

You see, once you've convinced yourself that trying new things will only end in embarrassment or painful failures, each new attempt at success then becomes tainted with discomfort and that glaring memory that's always blinking back at you in the rear-view mirror.

We can never look forward while we're always looking back. We can never expect to create new, positive outcomes if we're always playing out our old mistakes. You have to re-engage your imagination and start creating better ideals for those "what if" situations. Instead of fearing failure, we should allow our "what if" principals to let us see failure as experiments and opportunities to try again until we succeed.

Try using your pre-meditation time to play out a few different possibilities and outcomes that end in you feeling more confident and successful. Try thinking about the fact that you already possess all the energy you need to succeed in life; it's just waiting for your permission before it starts revealing itself.

Renew Your Self-Esteem and Self-Love with the Power of Your Mind
When it comes down to it, the present moment is all we have. To really start loving yourself, you have to be aware, awake, living in the here and in the now, looking for fulfillment in every moment.

In order to appreciate yourself and your life, accept what comes your way, totally and completely. Learn from mistakes and let them go.

At the end of the day, you are the judge of your worth, and your goal thus is to discover infinite worth in yourself, no matter what anyone else thinks!

Whether you love or loathe them, the people you react to most strongly are merely projections of your inner world. What you hate most about others are the aspects of yourself that you're in conflict with. What you love most about others are the aspects that you admire in yourself and invite into your life.

Exercise

In this exercise, I want you to take the time to make some new, empowering assumptions for your life. Take my examples, add some words here or there, and then recite, practice, and incorporate them into your daily life.

Your New Assumptions:

1. The physical world, including our bodies, is a response of the observer. I create my own body as I create the experience of my world.

2. My body is - in its essential state - composed of energy and information, not merely solid matter. The energy and information I have within my body offers infinite opportunities for success and happiness.

3. My mind and my body are one. I am made up out of streams of thoughts, feelings, and desires, but I also feel on a physical level. Physical and emotional experiences come together to form a single creative source.

4. Perception is a learned phenomenon and the world I live in is dictated by how I learned to perceive it. If I can change my perception, I can change my experience.

5. I am not a victim of sickness or my circumstances. Those aspects are part of the scenery, not of me. I am a free spirit, and if I chose to accept it, I can and will start loving myself for all that I am.

"We begin to find and become ourselves when we notice how we are already found, already truly, entirely, wildly, messily, marvelously who we were meant to be." – Anne Lamott

CHAPTER 11

How to Raise Your Vibrational Frequency and Transform Your Life

It's not uncommon to look at those around you and think that they seem to have it all. Their lives seem perfect, and they just seem to have a lot of luck in general.

In my personal opinion, I think that in most instances, it's NOT about luck, but rather about energy, our personal power, our ability to attract into our lives that which we manifest, that we deserve, and feel worthy of.

I know that I've been flat on the floor due to seriously low vibrational energy. I felt stuck with no idea how to move forward. I was crippled by limiting beliefs that were holding me back no end.

As you know by now, it's something I was able to overcome. I now have my health back, I have a deep love for myself, and I have an amazing life. I have managed to free myself from the fear and limiting beliefs, and I'm proud to say that I have some of the most amazing friends. But none of it would have been possible if I didn't focus on raising my vibrational energy and keeping it up there.

Fundamentally, I learned how to let go of the need to know how everything would play out; I simply trusted that in the end, it would work out.

What is vibration?
Cassandra Sturdy describes it like this: *"Your 'vibration' is a fancy way of describing your overall state of being. Everything in the universe is made up of energy vibrating at different frequencies. Even things that look solid are made up of vibrational energy fields at the quantum level. This includes you."*

When you look at vibration from a metaphysical perspective, we are all beings that are made up of different energy levels: physical, mental, emotional, and spiritual. Each of those levels has their own vibrational frequency, and when combined, they create our overall vibration of being.

Vibrations operate at high or low frequencies that exist within and around us. If your vibration is low, it's pretty easy to spot; it's just a matter of bringing awareness to your situation and then working on rectifying it.

Let's suppose that you're having a hard time with finances. Or your health isn't exactly what it needs to be. Or you've got a bunch of toxic, crappy friends that surround you all day, every day. That's when your vibration tends to be low. And that's exactly when you need to work on fixing it and raising it to where it needs to be again.

On the other hand, if your vibration is high, you get a beautiful sense of a life that's just flowing in all the right ways. When your vibration is high, you begin to experience things like meeting inspiring people, jumping out of bed in the morning when you're filled with optimism. You might be having great success at work, or perhaps your bank balance hasn't looked this good in like forever!

When your vibrational energy is high, others might think that you have all the luck in the world, but in fact, you've created your own outcomes by working hard on your energy.

Energies tend to attract to likewise energies. When my vibration is low, all areas of my life are affected by it. If my vibration is high, all aspects of my life benefit from it.

So how can you raise your vibration? It sounds super complex, but when you look at the techniques you're about to discover, you'll see that it can be the simplest of activities that can help you raise and keep your vibrational energy as high as possible!

My good friend and mentor, Mark Anastasi, has been studying holistic health and alternative healing for what seems to be a lifetime. He has helped countless people align their thoughts and their actions to essentially transform their lives, which is why I feel it only makes sense to include some of his teachings in this book.

I sat down with Mark and asked him about what his thoughts were on vibrational energy, and how we could all use it to help us transform our lives for the better. Here's what he had to say:

15 Proven Ways to Harness the Power of Raised Vibrational Energy and Totally Transform Your Life

1. Start by Loving Yourself
The number one thing you must do in order to move forward in life, and raise your vibrational frequency, is to love yourself. This is not always an easy thing to do, yet it is a crucial first step if you want to improve your life. You must accept yourself for who and what you are. We really have to make peace with ourselves.

2. Love Others
Be more loving, understanding, and forgiving towards others. People who love themselves are usually very caring, generous and kind to others too; they express their self-confidence through humility, forgiveness, and inclusiveness. Do something for someone else. Meet up with a friend. Hug some people. Play with puppies. Ask yourself: "What would love do now?"

Studies have proven that doing something kind for people produces a reduction in feelings of depression, hostility, isolation, and helplessness, and enhanced feelings of joy, self-worth, emotional resilience and optimism. Interestingly, observing an act of kindness or generosity also releases endorphins in people's bloodstreams and makes them feel great!

If love is indeed the great unifying energy that makes up our Universe, it stands to reason that acting in accordance with our true nature (love) would produce feelings of wellbeing in us.

> *"We feel greater self-worth and more successful when we provide services for others. There's a touch of the Good Samaritan in all of us. Therefore, there is wisdom in setting aside a special time in our daily routines for doing something that helps another person. The only thing that truly satisfies the soul is love and appreciation, and when we feel and express these feelings, we feel fulfilled."*
>
> *– Dr. John Demartini*

Another study shows that smiling can actually decrease stress enhancing hormones such as cortisol, adrenaline, and dopamine, and can increase the level of mood-enhancing hormones such as endorphins. Smiling has also been found to reduce one's overall blood pressure.

The positive mental, physical, and emotional effects experienced by kindhearted individuals encompass an extremely broad realm. For instance, such individuals have more fulfilling relationships, a lower divorce rate, a stronger sense of spirituality, relief from anxiety and depression, deep feelings of self-worth, jobs they love and live longer lives.

> *"You do not have to know the who, what, where, when and how what you want, it is going to happen. Your job is to be A CREATOR, to decree, to send out the blueprints into the fields of existence, and to do so consciously, with grace, with creativity, with bravado and courage. And a little bit of*

humility does you a lot of good, and GRATITUDE always does you the BEST of good. Always offer your gratitude, and your consciousness will grow in immense leaps and bounds. Always express your GRATITUDE every day. All of this is felt."

– Barbara Marciniak

3. Be Grateful

Be grateful for who you are, what you have, and what you are experiencing – and have experienced in the past. Be grateful for your powers of creation. Be grateful for your goals and visions that are yet to occur in your reality. That is the mindset you need in order to manifest more abundance in your life.

Focusing on what you are grateful for is one of the most powerful ways to elevate your vibrational frequency.

If you write down 20 things you are grateful for, and 20 things you are proud of, it helps shift your energy considerably. I know how much it helped me. You can choose to focus on 'what is wrong with you,' or you can focus on your positive goals, affirmations, the person you want to become, and what you have to be grateful for.

My advice: wake up in the morning and say "Thank You" for this brand new day.
Set a powerful intention for the day ("I'm having an AMAZING, SUPER-PRODUCTIVE, FUN DAY today!"; "A MIRACLE is going to happen in my life today!"). At night, before going to sleep, write down a 'quality question' on a notepad that you'll keep by your bed ("How can I complete this task and enjoy the process?"; "How can I earn a magnificent living doing what I love?"), and say "Thank you" once more, expressing gratitude for the things that occurred in your life that day.

4. Always Have Integrity at Heart

Be truthful and honest. The truth always raises your vibrational frequency. Lying and inauthenticity lowers it.

You clean up your life by living a life with a good moral compass, and by having integrity in all your daily activities. And if you haven't done so up until now, forgive yourself – and those that have trespassed against you – make the necessary rectifications, and start afresh.

5. Dissolve Your Fears

Nothing represses human potential and diminishes energy levels as living in fear and worry. Demonstrate courage and face your fears. And remember: it really doesn't matter what anyone else thinks. You don't need to win anybody's approval. Live your life on your terms. Dissolve fear through love. As Neale Donald Walsch puts it, "All human actions are motivated at their deepest level by one of two emotions – Love or Fear. Fear is the energy which contracts, closes down, draws in, runs, hides, hoards, harms. Love is the energy which expands, opens up, sends out, stays, reveals, shares, heals."

6. Move Your Body, Exercise

Research shows that walking 10% faster than usual with your head held high makes it impossible to feel depressed. Tell that to the $11-billion-a-year antidepressants industry!

Go for a walk, run, jump, dance, exercise… move your body! Our physiology is a wonderful tool for improving our mood, raising our energy level and vibrational frequency, not to mention it detoxifies the body. Ever felt unmotivated to go to the gym, but went anyway and felt energized after a good workout?

7. Laugh!

When you laugh, you strengthen your energy field, you strengthen your aura, and you strengthen your immune system. Remember: Truth, Love, and Joy are divine attitudes. Some people have laughed themselves into healing, and even cured themselves of cancer by watching funny movies (Norman Cousins claims to have cured himself of cancer through laughter therapy, watching funny films for 8 hours a day). "Laughter is a sign of an elevated spirit, laughter heals the body, and opens up the chakras to take healing energy inside," Barbara Marciniak points out.

8. Have Positive Thoughts, Use Positive Words

Positive thoughts and words raise your vibrational frequency, and negative ones drain you. When you wake up in the morning, set a positive intention: "I'm going to have an AMAZING day today!" And use affirmations daily! "I Am Amazing! I Am Inspiration! I Am Power!

Whenever you find yourself saying a negative statement about yourself or a situation, or thinking a negative thought, stop yourself, realize that words have a creative power to them (negative statements attract and manifest more negativity into your life), and come up with a more empowering and positive way to view the situation.

For example, when I catch myself thinking some particularly murderous thoughts about someone that wronged me, I place a brown 'X' through that visual image, and I look at the situation from a more detached, elevated perspective: why am I manifesting this situation? What is the lesson? What would love and understanding do now?

And, very important: cut your television viewing by at least 90%, and for the love of God stop watching and reading the news...

9. Surround Yourself with Positive People

The physical world is actually a vast system of energy. There is a subtle energy that flows between people. Have you ever noticed how you feel good around people who are loving, non-judgmental, positive, secure in themselves, with high self-esteem? And conversely, you feel tired and drained around other people?

Stay away from people who drain your energy! Many people feel insecure and weak, so they resort to shouting at you, swearing, causing conflict, bullying, putting you down, or simply having subtle digs at you and your appearance... in order to steal some of your energy and strengthen their own.

People who are on anti-depressants and other narcotics and that experience depressed lows to manic high are disconnected from the source of boundless energy – God-Mind, Source (the clue is in the name! ha!). This is why meditation has so many incredible benefits, by the way.

Call special friends or relatives who uplift your mood. Have fun! Organize fun days out with your – positive, loving – friends! This is another great way to connect with people, share laughter and fun, and it raises your vibrational frequency!

"Make sure you count your blessings. [...] Those who are grateful have more blessings and fulfillment in life than those who do not. This is a simple principle, yet it has the power to change your life. Gratitude is the key to growth and fulfillment. [...] True gratitude actually has little to do with those temporary moments of happiness or elation. True gratitude is a quiet state of poise and inner calm where you're truly thankful, where you sense the divine order and wouldn't want anything to change.

[...] As a result, you receive even more gifts. To those who are grateful, more is given. To those who are not, more is taken away. Having gifts taken away as a result of ingratitude helps you wake up to the importance of being grateful. Nothing has ever happened or can happen to you that is not a gift and a blessing, but it's difficult to be thankful until you find the hidden benefit in what may seem at first to be a negative event."

– Dr. John Demartini, The Breakthrough Experience

10. Do What You LOVE
Do something every day that makes you happy. Do the things you LOVE to do. Do the things that make you happy. Give lovingly.

When you live life on your terms, going after your purpose and your mission, you feel better about yourself. When you don't, not only does your body break down, but your mental state does as well.

Make a list of all the things that make you happy. And make a list of all the things that make you unhappy. Ask yourself why these things make you unhappy (usually it has something to do with your childhood). Work diligently to eliminate the things that make you feel unhappy and move towards realizing and experiencing regularly –

daily, even – the things that make you happy. Sounds simple enough, right?

Take time every day to do or experience something that makes you feel happy all the time. At least once per month, do something more special that makes you happy. And of course, what will make you most happy and contented with your life is when you listen to your heart and follow your true path in life, instead of doing things merely out of obligation or to please others.

11. Create Beauty; Surround Yourself with Beauty
Barbara Marciniak advises us to 'create beauty' in our lives. "Beauty opens our senses and makes us more psychic. That's the true meaning of Art. To make Beauty. And then to have that Beauty really stimulate our senses so that we can move beyond the reality we are in, and sense our connectedness to other realities because reality is multi-dimensional. Give reverence to the earth. Give thanks to all the elements. Do everything you can to honor. Honor with action, honor with vision, honor with words. Make beauty. Whether it's the way, you arrange your room.... so that you wake up and see beauty… or loving nature or making the land you are on more beautiful."

12. Connect With Nature

Connect with nature, every day. Walk barefoot in the grass, visit a park, go into the sea, spend twenty minutes in the sun… This helps align you with the Earth's natural resonance and raises your vibrational frequency.

13. Connect to Source (Meditate)
Your energy levels and vibrational frequency increase when you meditate regularly. The comedian Jerry Seinfeld once said: "More than money, more than love, more than just about anything, I love ENERGY. I love it, and I pursue it, and I want more of it. Physical and mental energy to me is the greatest riches of human life. And meditating is like this free account of an endless amount of energy."

14. Cleanse Your Body
Cut out processed foods, sugar, alcohol, soft drinks, bread, dairy products, pharmaceutical drugs, chemical beauty and cleaning products. Detox regularly, cleanse your body and eat living foods (organic sprouts, fruit, and vegetables). This will raise your vibrational frequency, energy, and vitality beyond anything you can imagine!

> *"You owe it to your physical self that when you get the privilege of growing one of these physical things you call a body... it's a miracle; you are spirit in body... to honor your body and eat well. Love the body that you have created. Work with it to bring it to its highest frequency."*
>
> Barbara Marciniak

15. Enjoy Loving Sex in a Beautiful Relationship
Yes, sex increases your vibrational frequency, when it is done lovingly!

Powerful Tips for Improving Self-Love

They say that nobody can go back and start a new beginning, but ANYONE can start today and make a new ending. This is so true, and I have personally learned, once you decide to take action and change your life and work on your self-love, there's really nothing that can stand in your way!

How we feel and what we think about ourselves, whether or not we accept ourselves, it all impacts how much we end up loving ourselves. Having a high opinion of yourself of who you are and loving every inch of your existence is one of the things that so many people don't allow themselves to do these days.

Here are some more powerful ways in which you can work on your love for yourself:

1. Stop the inner critic.
Learning to handle and replace the voice of your inner critic is a great place to start when it comes to improving self-love. We all have inner critics that can either spur us on to get things done or, if we allow it,

drag our self-love and self-esteem down. The inner voice might whisper, or it might shout thoughts like *"You're lazy and sloppy"* or *"You aren't good at your job"* or *"You are worse or uglier than your friends"*.

But just because the inner critic is thinking it, doesn't mean you have to accept it as true. Whenever you feel the inner critic coming alive, try using a stop-word or a stop-phrase, something you can do aloud or even just in your mind. Whenever the critic starts with its crap, just shout or say to yourself STOP. You can also come up with a phrase or a word that will lead your inner critic off that specific train of thought and get it to focus on the good things in life.

2. Get used to using healthier motivation habits.
You have to motivate yourself to take action and raise your self-esteem and self-love levels, and by using healthy motivation habits, it'll be that much easier to do. You can try writing down the deeply felt benefits you'll get from following your new path or reaching a specific goal. Nothing motivates us more than writing our goals down! You can also try setting goals and including things that you'd really love to do, things that drive you, that put a smile on your face, that charges and drives you in life.

3. Take a few appreciation breaks every day.
This is a simple but fun and powerful way of working on your self-love and self-esteem on a daily basis. If you end up spending just two minutes a day, being thankful and appreciating all the good things in your life, at least you've spent 2% of your day on positive thoughts that help build you as a person. Take a deep breath, slow down and ask yourself this question: what are 3 things I can appreciate about myself?
A few examples that have come up when I have used this exercise are that I:
- Help quite a few people each day through what I write.
- Can make people laugh and forget about their troubles.
- Am very thoughtful and caring when it comes to my friends and colleagues.

These things don't have to be big things. Maybe just that you listened fully for a few minutes to someone who needed it today. That you took a healthy walk or bike ride after work. That you are a caring and kind person in many situations. These short breaks do not only build self-esteem in the long run but can also turn a negative mood around and reload you with a lot of positive energy again.

4. Write down 3 things in the evening that you can appreciate about yourself.

This is a variation of the habit above and combining the two of them can be extra powerful for two boosts in self-esteem a day.
Or you may simply prefer to use this variation at the end of your day when you have some free time for yourself to spare.
What you do is to ask yourself the question from the last section:
What are 3 things I can appreciate about myself?
Write down your answers every evening in a journal made out of paper or on your computer/smart phone.
A nice extra benefit of writing it down is that after a few weeks you can read through all the answers to get a good self-esteem boost and change in perspective on days when you may need it the most.

5. Do the right thing.

When you do what you deep down think is the right thing to do then you raise and strengthen your self-esteem. It might be a small thing like getting up from the couch and going to the gym. It could be to be understanding instead of judgmental in a situation. Or to stop feeling sorry for yourself and focus on the opportunities and gratitude for what you actually have. It is not always easy to do. Or even to know what the right thing is. But keeping a focus on it and doing it as best you can makes a big difference both in the results you get and for how you think about yourself.
One tip that makes it easier to stay consistent with doing the right thing is to try to take a few such actions early in the day. Like for example giving someone a compliment, eating a healthy breakfast and working out. This sets the tone for the rest of your day.

6. Replace the perfectionism.

Few thought habits can be so destructive in daily life as perfectionism. It can paralyze you from taking action because you become so afraid

of not living up to some standard. And so you procrastinate and you do not get the results you want. This will make your self-esteem sink. Or you take action but are never or very rarely satisfied with what you accomplished and your own performance. And so your opinion and feelings about yourself become more and more negative and your motivation to take action plummets. How can you overcome perfectionism?
A few things that really helped me are:
- Go for good enough. When you aim for perfection then that usually winds up in a project or a task never being finished. So simply go for good enough instead. Don't use it as an excuse to slack off. But simply realize that there is something called good enough and when you are there then you are finished.
- Remember that buying into myths of perfection will hurt you and the people in your life. This simple reminder that life is not like in a movie, a song or a book can be a good reality check whenever you are daydreaming of perfection. Because reality can clash with your expectations when they are out of this world and harm or even possibly lead to the end of relationships, jobs, projects and so on.

7. Handle mistakes and failures in a more positive way.
If you go outside of your comfort zone, if you try to accomplish anything that is truly meaningful then you could stumble and fall along the way.
And that is OK. It is normal. It is what people that did something that truly mattered have done throughout all ages. Even if we don't always hear about it as much as we hear about their successes.
So remember that. And when you stumble try this:
- Be your own best friend. Instead of beating yourself up, ask yourself: How would my friend/parent support me and help me in this situation? Then do things and talk to yourself like he or she would. It keeps you from falling into a pit of despair and helps you to be more constructive after the first initial pain of a mistake or failure starts to dissipate.
- Find the upside. Another way to be more constructive in this kind of situation is to focus on optimism and opportunities. So ask yourself: what is one thing I can learn from this? And what

is one opportunity I can find in this situation? This will help you to change your viewpoint and hopefully not hit the same bump a little further down the road.

8. Be kinder towards other people.
When you are kinder towards others you tend to treat and think of yourself in a kinder way too. And the way you treat other people is how they tend to treat you in the long run.
So focus on being kind in your daily life.
You can for example:
- Just be there and listen as you let someone vent.
- Hold open the door for the next person.
- Let someone into your lane while driving.
- Encourage a friend or a family member when they are uncertain or unmotivated.
- Take a few minutes to help someone out in a practical way.

9. Try something new.
When you try something new, when you challenge yourself in a small or bigger way and go outside of your comfort zone then your opinion of yourself goes up.
You may not have done whatever you did in a spectacular or great way but you at least tried instead of sitting on your hands and doing nothing.
And that is something to appreciate about yourself and it can help you come alive as you get out of a rut. So go outside of your comfort zone regularly. Don't expect anything, just tell yourself that you will try something out.
And then later on you can do the same thing a few more times and improve your own performance. And as always, if it feels too scary or uncomfortable then don't beat yourself up. Take a smaller step forward instead by gently nudging yourself into motion.

10. Stop falling into the comparison trap.
When you compare your life, yourself and what you have to other people's lives and what they have then you have a destructive habit on your hands.

Because you can never win. There is always someone who has more or is better than you at something in the world. There are always people ahead of you.
So replace that habit with something better.
Look at how far you have come so far instead. Compare yourself to yourself. Focus on you. On your results. And on how you can and how you have improved your results. This will both motivate you and raise your self-esteem.

11. Spend more time with supportive people (and less time with destructive people).

Even if you focus on being kinder towards other people (and yourself) and on replacing a perfectionism habit it will be hard to keep your self-esteem up if the most important influences in your life drag it down on a daily or weekly basis.
So make changes in the input you get. Choose to spend less time with people who are nervous perfectionists, unkind or unsupportive of your dreams or goals. And spend more time with positive, uplifting people who have more human and kinder standards and ways of thinking about things.
And think about what you read, listen to and watch too. Spend less time on an internet forum, reading a magazine or watching a TV-show if you feel it makes you unsure of yourself and if it makes you feel more negatively towards yourself.
Then spend the time you used to spend on this information source on, for example, reading books, blogs, websites and listening to podcasts that help you and that make you feel good about yourself.

12. Remember the why's of high self-esteem.

What is a simple way to stay consistent with doing something? As mentioned above: to remember the most important reasons why you are doing it.
So remind yourself of the why's at the start of this article to help yourself to stay motivated to work on your self-esteem and to make it an essential priority.

"Don't rely on someone else for your happiness and self-worth. Only you can be responsible for that. If you can't love and respect yourself – no one else will be able to make that happen. Accept who you are – completely; the good and the bad – and make changes as YOU see fit – not because you think someone else wants you to be different."
– Stacey Charter

Conclusion

This concludes 'The Seven Steps to Finally Loving Yourself.' I sincerely hope that you have enjoyed reading it and that you have already started putting what you've learned here into practice.

Remember, the seven secrets to truly loving yourself are:

- Follow your life purpose to live an authentic life

- Cut out media to achieve a deeper self-love

- Identify and eliminate all your limiting beliefs

- Stop believing advertisements, they curb your self-love

- What you eat contributes to your levels of self-love

- Always take care of your mind, body, and soul

- Meditate often!

Masters practice the fundamentals over and over again. Make sure you do the exercises in the book, and I promise you, you'll be amazed at the impact it will have on your life and on your level of self-love.

I feel privileged to have had the opportunity of inspiring you with my words, and I wish you nothing but the best on your journey ahead.

Remember: Life is for living!
You are already unstoppable
You have already achieved success
And you are already well on your way towards achieving your dreams
You just haven't realized it yet, and you should, because you're amazing and deserve to love yourself at the deepest level possible!

I love my community members. If you have a story or something inspirational to share, please do let me know. As well as offering Self-Esteem Coaching, I also offer Anti-Ageing Coaching, whereby we work on strengthening the things that can prematurely age you, for example meeting your emotional, mental and physical needs to bring out the beautiful you, so feel free to get in touch with me via email contact@laurelleburghamcoaching.com and feel free to look at my website www.laurelleburghamcoaching.com

I look forward to hearing from you
Elle xxx

www.ingramcontent.com/pod-product-compliance
Lightning Source LLC
Chambersburg PA
CBHW070154100426
42743CB00013B/2907